T
e
r

V
c
v
c
b
w
d
c

F
n
p
a
info@howtobooks.co.uk

The Publishers
www.howtobooks

If your want to know how . . .

Practical Research Methods
A user-friendly, six stage guide to mastering research

Critical Thinking for Students
Learn the skills of critical assessment and effective argument

Writing an Assignment
Proven techniques from a chief examiner that really get results

Writing Your Dissertation
*The bestselling guide to planning, preparing and presenting
first-class work*

howtobooks

Please send for a free copy of the latest catalogue to:
How To Books
3 Newtec Place, Magdalen Road
Oxford OX4 1RE, United Kingdom
e-mail: info@howtobooks.co.uk
www.howtobooks.co.uk

Returning to Education

A practical handbook for adult learners

DR CATHERINE DAWSON

howtobooks

Published by How To Books Ltd,
3 Newtec Place, Magdalen Road,
Oxford OX4 1RE, United Kingdom.
Tel: (01865) 793806. Fax: (01865) 248780.
e-mail: info@howtobooks.co.uk
http://www.howtobooks.co.uk

British Library Cataloguing in Publication Data.
A catalogue record for this book is available from
the British Library.

Produced for How To Books by Deer Park Productions
Typeset by Kestrel Data, Exeter, Devon
Cover design by Baseline Arts Ltd, Oxford
Printed and bound by Cromwell Press Ltd, Trowbridge, Wiltshire

NOTE: The material contained in this book is set out in good
faith for general guidance and no liability can be accepted
for loss or expense incurred as a result of relying in particular
circumstances on statements made in the book. Laws and
regulations are complex and liable to change, and readers should
check the current position with the relevant authorities before
making personal arrangements.

Contents

Preface

This book is aimed at adults who have spent some time away from the education system who now wish to return to learning.

It covers all aspects of the returning process, from a description of the types of courses, institutions and qualifications available to advice about the financial support offered to adults.

Also covered in the book are some of the more personal and social issues that affect adults returning to education, such as how to cope with change and fitting learning in with other demands on time.

I have been a researcher and tutor working with adult learners for 15 years. All the examples and quotations used in this book have been gathered over that time and during the research for my doctorate. It never fails to amaze me how important returning to education can be – what a life-changing event it can be for many adults.

You have picked up this book and, therefore, must be thinking about returning to education. For many people it can be a daunting process and you may be undecided about whether it is the right decision for you. By reading this book you will increase your understanding of the education system and begin to address the issues that may be concerning you. This will help you to make up your mind about when and how to return to learning.

Once you have made your decision I hope that you find it a rewarding and fulfilling experience, as have so many adults over the years.

Dr Catherine Dawson

(1)

Reasons for Returning

There are many different reasons why adults decide to return to education. It could be that you are experiencing some type of life transition – children might be going to school or retirement age might be approaching quickly. Or perhaps you feel that you have missed out on educational opportunities in the past and know that you are capable of much more than you are achieving at present.

When you consider returning to education you need to think about the reasons *why* you want to return to learning as these will have an influence on what, when and how to study. Today there is a wide selection of courses, qualifications and subject areas open to adults and offered by a variety of learning providers. Different courses and institutions will suit different circumstances and personalities. By under-standing your initial reasons for returning to learning, you will be able to consider courses and institutions that are the most appropriate for you.

This chapter will help you to consider your reasons for returning in more depth. Chapters 2 and 3 provide an up-to-date description of the different courses, subject areas, institutions, qualifications and mode of study to help you with your learning choices.

WHY DO I WANT TO RETURN TO LEARNING?

When you are thinking about returning to education, it is useful to ask yourself why you want to return to learning. Adults return to education for a multitude of reasons and these different reasons will have an influence on what is studied, as the following examples illustrate:

Tina (31)

My son is 4 years old and starts school in September. I've been thinking for a while that I'm going to have time on my hands, you know, I'm not going to have him pulling at my skirt all the time going 'mum do this, or mum do that'. So I thought I've got loads of time in the day to do something and I didn't get many qualifications at school so I thought it might be a good idea to do something with this time. But the problem is I've got to pick him up from school at 3.15pm and I can't drop him until 8.30am so I need something that will fit in with that. And also if he's poorly in the day I've got to have something that will let me go and get him. I don't want to get behind with my work so it's got to be really flexible.

Roy (57)

I had an accident at work four years ago so I'm on sick pay. I know I'm not going to be able to work again. It's a right shock when that happens. I was wallowing in self-pity for a quite a while, but now I've decided I've got to do something as otherwise I'll just waste away. I was watching a programme the other day about old houses and how to identify old features and find out their age. I was fascinated and I wondered if I could go to college and study something about that. I have a problem with getting around though, so I don't know if I will be able to do it. Also I'm getting on a bit, I don't know if they want people like me in their places nowadays.

Andrew (28)

I'm sick to death of work. The people I work with, well, I just don't get on with them. We've got nothing in common, you know? I really do think I can do better than this. The problem was I were a bit naughty at school, it weren't that I weren't clever, I just messed around, you know? So I never got any exams and all that. So if I don't want to go mad I've got to do something. I've got a mate who went to university and he got on really well. I reckon I can do that, you know? Where I come from there's nowt better than a degree. If I got that I could do something else with my life, you know?

Example 1 – Tina

Tina is expecting a change in her life which will free up her time during the day. Although she hopes to have between six and seven hours a day free, she knows that she may have to look after her son if he has to come home from school early.

There are a variety of options open to Tina and, in addition to thinking about why she wants to return to education, she will need to think carefully about what interests her and also consider her particular personality traits. For example, she might want to consider an access course aimed specifically at women. Some of these are taught during the day while children are at school. The courses are flexible and tutors understand if time has to be taken off to look after children. As they are attended by other women in similar positions, there is plenty of peer support available.

Some access courses offer a variety of subjects within the course. These are best described as 'tasters' which are especially useful for people who are unsure about which subjects interest them. Other options available to Tina include correspondence courses or internet learning, both of which can be done at home at her own pace (see Chapter 2). However, she will need to decide whether she has the motivation to work on her own or whether she would prefer to work with others.

Example 2 – Roy

Roy is concerned about personal mobility problems and the fact that staff and students at colleges may not want older students with disabilities on the course. Although older buildings in some institutions are difficult to access, modern buildings tend to be built with mobility difficulties in mind. Some have wheelchair access and are on the ground floor in light, airy premises. Roy would need to check that his class was accessible in terms of physical access before enrolling. Otherwise, he too could consider learning opportunities available in the home.

Like many adults returning to education, Roy is concerned also about his age. However, the type of course he is talking about would tend to be run by an adult education department of a university or by a further education college. It would be part-time, probably run during the evening. Most, if not all of the students on this course would be mature students, with many over retirement age, so Roy would certainly not be out of place.

There are, however, some courses and institutions which tend to market themselves at younger students. These are easily spotted – they will specify a minimum amount of A Levels or GCSEs required for entry; they will emphasise the 'fun' aspects of study that appeals to 18-years old – the nightlife, the number of bars, rag week pranks, etc. However, mature students do go to this type of institution and do fit in well. You need to think about the learning environment in which you would feel most comfortable. If you think you would feel out of place in this type of environment, choose something else.

Today there are many institutions aimed specifically at adults. Even within some of the more traditional universities there are adult education departments, some of which, you might be surprised to hear, have an average age of student which is well over retirement age. Other institutions, such as the newer universities and many colleges, now have more mature students than 18-year-old students, so 'fitting in' really should not be a problem. If you want to concentrate on your studies rather than worry about fitting in, find somewhere to study that is aimed at people like yourself. These will be described in depth in Chapter 2.

Example 3 – Andrew
In the final example, Andrew has his heart set on obtaining a

degree. He has a young family and needs to study close to home. In his home town there are two universities – one used to be a polytechnic, but became a university in 1994. This institution now has more mature student entrants than 18-year-old entrants. However, the traditional, red brick university in his town makes entry hard for people without high A Level grades. Another option open to Andrew would be to study for a degree with the Open University which would allow him to study at home at his own pace (see Chapter 2). However, he thinks that he would not have the discipline or enough quiet time to study at home and feels, therefore, that he would like to study at the more welcoming university.

When you are thinking about why you want to return to education you need to think about your personal circumstances, interests, likes and dislikes as all of these will have an influence on what and where to study. In the above examples, people are able to express some of these clearly, but others might be hidden and only become apparent with careful thought and analysis. The following lists may help you to consider some of these issues.

PERSONAL CIRCUMSTANCES

◆ Are you single or do you have a partner to consider? Will they be supportive or oppose your plans? Will they be threatened by your decision to return to learning?

◆ Do you have children? Is there someone else available to look after them should they become ill?

◆ Do you have any other caring responsibilities that have to be taken into account?

◆ Do you have any friends who will be supportive of your plans or might they put obstacles in your way? Have any of your friends returned to education and could they offer advice and help, should it be required?

◆ Will your work colleagues and your boss be supportive? Will they allow time off for study if required?

◆ What are your financial circumstances? Can you afford to give up paid employment, or do you need to continue earning? Do you have a reliable source of finance if you're not working?

◆ How much of your present lifestyle do you want to change, or are you prepared to change, for your learning?

◆ Is something likely to happen in your life which might affect your ability to continue studying?

◆ Are you able to attend a course for regular hours and on regular days of a week or will you require something more flexible?

◆ Can you commit to the required level of time needed for your course?

◆ Will you be able to find some quiet time at home to complete your coursework? Is there a comfortable, quiet place available in which to work?

PERSONAL CHARACTERISTICS AND INTERESTS

◆ Do you prefer to study on your own initiative or is the support of others important to you?

◆ Do you prefer to study on your own or is face-to-face contact important to you? Do you like to work in groups?

◆ How do you cope if faced with strict deadlines set by others? Would you prefer to work at your own pace and set your own deadlines?

◆ How do you feel about exams? Do they fill you with dread or do you take them in your stride? Would you prefer a different type of assessment?

◆ Do you like listening to lectures or are experimentation and discussion important to you?

◆ Are qualifications important to you or are you interested in learning without obtaining qualifications?

◆ Do you prefer individual competition or working together towards a common goal?

◆ Do you get on with people of all ages or would you prefer to mix with people of similar ages?

◆ Do you prefer to mix with people from similar backgrounds or from different backgrounds?

◆ Do you have any negative perceptions which are putting you off returning to learning? (These will be discussed in more depth in Chapter 7.)

As a final note, some adults have bad memories of school and education. However, most adults who return to education stress how surprised they are that it is not like school. They find that tutors respect them, valuing their knowledge and experience; adults learn from each other; classes are informal; tutors and students become friends; teaching methods are very different, aimed at, and suited to, adult learners and nothing like they were at school. All these factors lead to an enjoyable and rewarding experience. By taking your time to choose an appropriate course and learning provider, you too should find that returning to education can be an exciting, rewarding and important decision in your life.

SUMMARY

There are many different reasons why adults decide to return to education, for example:

◆ You are experiencing a life transition:
   —children approaching school age
   —retirement approaching
   —significant age approaching.

◆ You have missed out on educational opportunities in the past.

◆ You know that you are capable of more.

◆ You want to show what you are worth.

◆ You are stuck in a rut:
  —unhappy in work
  —unhappy at home
  —career going nowhere.

◆ You want to increase your earning potential.

◆ You want to increase the job choices open to you.

◆ You want to make new friends and acquaintances.

◆ You want to develop your interests.

◆ You want to develop your intellect.

◆ You want to keep your brain active.

You need to think very carefully about why you want to return to education as this will influence what, when and where to study. You also need to think about your personal characteristics, likes, dislikes and interests when you choose what to study as this will help keep your motivation levels high.

2

Learning Options

Over recent years the concept of lifelong learning has become increasingly popular. The government believes that education should be available to all adults who want to learn and who can benefit in some way from that learning. As a consequence, a number of new initiatives have been developed which should make the learning process easier for adults. In this chapter some of these initiatives are outlined, along with some of the older, popular courses and institutions, so that you can begin to understand what is on offer for you within the different sectors of the education system.

COURSES FOR ADULTS

Throughout the UK there are many courses aimed specifically at adults. These courses are designed and taught with your interests and concerns at the forefront. This means that tutors realise that your circumstances are different to those of school leavers and they will be more flexible and understanding, helping you through any difficulties you may encounter. For example, they may provide extra help for study skills or be more understanding if you have to miss a class due to childcare commitments.

Access courses

These courses are for adults who are interested in returning to learning after having had a period away from the education system. Some are aimed specifically at women. Access courses tend to follow one discipline, such as 'social sciences' or 'sciences', but within that discipline you usually get the opportunity to try out different subjects. For example, in a social sciences access course you might be able to study sociology, psychology, social policy, welfare rights and counselling skills. This is useful if you are not sure about what you want to study as it gives you the chance to 'taste' the subjects before making any final decisions. Many access courses are designed to help you get back into learning and will also offer help with your study skills.

Most access courses tend to be offered by further education colleges although some might be offered by higher education institutions or adult residential colleges (see below). Some colleges have joined together with local universities to offer a number of places on degree courses upon successful completion of the access course.

All access courses vary, so if you are interested in following this route you need to find out which subjects are on offer, how many you are required to study and whether places are available at your local university upon completion of your course. Contact your local college or ring learndirect (0800 100 900) to find out where access courses are run in your area. Some courses might be free, others attract a student bursary and some will give fee concessions for those on low incomes (see Chapters 5 and 6 and check with your chosen institution for more information).

University adult education departments

Some universities have adult education departments which are as old as the university itself. These go by many different names such as extra-mural departments, adult continuing education, and so on. These departments tend to offer short courses for adults in what used to be termed 'liberal' areas such as writing, painting, geology and so on. Others offer courses leading to professional qualifications, especially at postgraduate level.

If you live near a university ring the university enquiries number in your local telephone directory and ask if they have an adult education department. If they do you will be given a direct number. Ring and ask for a prospectus. Other departments have 'drop-in' centres where the information is readily available, usually in the form of leaflets, booklets or advice from the staff. Fees are payable – it is unlikely you will obtain financial support for this type of study although universities tend to offer fee concessions for those on low incomes.

Adult education service

Many county councils run their own adult education service. These provide courses aimed specifically at adults. Some may lead to vocational qualifications, others to academic qualifications, or many courses are offered for interest. For example, you might be interested in yoga for health, writing for profit or bricklaying. You have to pay for the courses although concessions are available for those on low incomes.

In some counties the adult education service runs 'bite size' or 'taster courses'. These are often free and provide an opportunity to try out the course before enrolling and paying a fee. Look in the *Yellow Pages* under 'adult education' or 'further education', or contact you local Citizen's Advice Bureau or County Council to find out about your local service. Many areas provide a free prospectus delivered to your home or made available in the local library.

Adult residential colleges

Throughout the country there are a number of adult residential colleges. These specialise in offering both short- and long-term courses for adults in a supportive, residential environment. Most colleges define adults as over the age of 21 and some will not offer places to anyone who has already got higher education qualifications.

Eight of the colleges offer long-term courses similar to access courses – they are designed to help adults get back into education, helping with study skills and providing the opportunity to study a variety of subjects before choosing your specific options. Bursaries are available for adults who wish to study on these long-term courses (see Chapter 6) and free accommodation, childcare and meals are also provided. Some colleges help with transport arrangements and costs. The colleges have made arrangements with local universities to offer a number of degree course places for those having successfully completed their course.

Adult residential colleges also offer short courses, usually over a period of two days to a week. There is a wide range of short course subjects on offer and these vary between colleges – some specialise in arts subjects, others in social and community issues, others in information technology.

Some colleges offer free accommodation and meals to students on short courses. In these colleges students learn from the tutors and from each other – living at the college is part of the learning experience. I have carried out evaluation research with students from one of these colleges for the past seven years and the feedback is always extremely positive.

To obtain a list of adult residential colleges offering short courses, contact:

Adult Residential Colleges Association (ARCA), PO Box 31, Washbrook, Ipswich, Suffolk, IP8 3HP. www.aredu.org.uk

The ARCA website contains a map of the UK with a list of all the adult residential colleges offering short courses. Click on the college in which you are interested and contact details and a description of each will appear.

To find out about the residential colleges offering long-term courses read Chapter 6 in which contact details for each college are provided. Telephone or write for a prospectus.

Workers' Educational Association

The Workers' Educational Association (WEA) is a registered charity, founded in 1903. It aims to provide high quality learning opportunities for adults from all walks of life, but especially those who may have missed out on learning in early life, or who are socially and economically disadvantaged. It is a national voluntary organisation that provides courses on a wide range of subjects for more than 100,000 students a year. It is recognised and financially supported by central and local government. The WEA is non-party political and works closely with a range of partners including Local Education Authorities, universities and other voluntary and community organisations.

Courses are organised by over 600 local branches throughout the UK. The WEA's **community learning provision** focuses on the needs of particular groups in the community, whereas the **workplace learning provision** recruits students in partnership with trades unions and employers. This initiative, in particular, caters for the needs of low-paid workers and those without formal qualifications. For details about courses, contact the WEA or visit their website.

WEA, Temple House, 17 Victoria Park Square, London E2 9PB. Tel: (020) 8983 1515. www.wea.org.uk

WEA Scottish Association, Riddle's Court, 322 Lawnmarket, Edinburgh EH1 2PG. Tel: (0131) 226 2345.

FURTHER EDUCATION COURSES

As an adult you can study at further education colleges. 'Further education' refers to any education which is undertaken after the compulsory school-leaving age. Broadly speaking there are five different types of institution offering further education:

◆ **General FE colleges** – these offer a wide range of courses to students of all ages, with most over the age of 19. Courses can be during the day, during the evening, full-time, part-time, day release or block release. Qualifications can be academic or vocational.

◆ **Sixth form colleges** – these are designed for 16-18 year olds and tend to be attached to schools.

◆ **Tertiary or community colleges** tend to fall somewhere between the above two FE providers. They have a greater number of younger students, although they also cater for older students, offering a wide variety of academic and vocational qualifications.

◆ **Agricultural colleges** – although these used to concentrate on purely agricultural areas such as farming and horticulture, they now offer related courses in areas such as business and engineering.

◆ **Specialist colleges** – throughout the country there are a number of colleges that specialise in offering further education in specific areas such as art and design, music or childcare.

In further education colleges some courses are more popular with 16-18 year-old students, such as those carried out full-time, during the day that lead to specific qualifications in popular subject areas. Some adults prefer not to study in this type of environment. If you find a course in which you are interested, you can always talk to guidance staff or tutors at the college to find out more about your fellow students. Evening classes and part-time courses tend, as a general rule, to be attended by adults rather than school leavers.

Many further education colleges will run courses designed specifically for adult learners. These could be access courses (see above) or might be foundation courses which are similar to access courses. This type of course comes under many different names, for example it might be called 'Fresh Start' or 'Springboard'. Again, all these courses will be designed for adults who have had a period of time away from education and who might be unsure about their ability to study or unclear about which subjects to study. The courses offer the chance to try out different subject areas within a supportive, adult environment.

If you are interested in finding out more about your further education college, look in the *Yellow Pages* under 'further education'. Ring the switchboard and ask for a prospectus or further details of courses on offer. If you are interested in courses aimed specifically at adults, say so and ask for further details. Most further education colleges will have advice and guidance workers or drop-in centres where you can obtain more details (see Chapter 4).

HIGHER EDUCATION COURSES

Higher education refers to education carried out at a level higher than A Levels or Level 3. It tends to be delivered in universities or colleges of higher education, although some further education colleges and adult residential colleges may offer some higher education courses. Polytechnics no longer exist – they were able to apply for university status from 1992.

At this present time there is talk of university mergers. However, in 2003, higher education institutions can be divided into ten categories:

1. The two old English universities of Oxford and Cambridge – a distinguishing feature is the college system.
2. The older Scottish universities of St Andrews, Edinburgh, Aberdeen and Glasgow, established in the thirteenth–fifteenth centuries.
3. The Universities of London and Wales which are made up of a number of specialist institutions.
4. The 'modern' or 'civic' universities established in the nineteenth and early twentieth centuries such as the University of Birmingham and the University of Sheffield. These are sometimes referred to as 'traditional' universities.
5. The 'new' universities which were built in the 1960s such as Kent and York.
6. The universities with technological roots such as Surrey and Loughborough.
7. The Open University (see below).
8. The former polytechnics which were granted university status by the Further and Higher Education Act 1992. These historically have close links with business and industry.
9. The privately funded University of Buckingham.
10. Higher education colleges.

Today, higher education institutions are increasingly diverse in their missions and provision of programmes of study. Generally, however, in higher education institutions you can study for degrees, diplomas or postgraduate qualifications, which refer to any qualifications higher than the level of degree, such as Master's degrees or Doctorates.

Universities are autonomous bodies that make their own decisions about selection criteria. Even today, some universities are very 'traditional' in terms of who they accept on their courses. Some ask for very high A Level grades and rarely consider offering places to people with other qualifications. If you are considering studying for a degree it will become quite obvious which universities are less open to 'non-traditional' students – look in your local library at various prospectuses and you will soon see.

Other universities, however, are much more adult friendly. They will accept people from access courses or other foundation courses. Some will accept your prior experience in a job as suitability for entry. By flicking through university prospectuses in your local library, or by visiting individual websites, you will find out which universities are more adult friendly.

When you are applying for a degree course at university, you do not apply to the individual institution. Instead, all applications for full-time undergraduate courses are dealt with by the Universities and Colleges Admissions Service (UCAS). If you enrol on an access course, your tutor will help you with the application procedure. Otherwise, application forms can be obtained from schools, colleges or from UCAS:

UCAS, Rosehill, New Barn Lane, Cheltenham, Gloucester-shire GL52 3LZ. Tel: (01242) 227788 (applicant enquiries and application procedures).

When you fill in an application form you will need to enter the code of your university choices. These codes are contained in the *UCAS Directory* which is produced annually and held by school, college and local libraries. When you request an application form you will be sent a booklet which outlines the application procedure. Soon you will be able to apply on-line through their website www.ucas.com although you will need to do this through an organisation such as a school or college which has registered with UCAS.

DISTANCE LEARNING/CORRESPONDENCE COURSES

Distance learning, sometimes called correspondence learning or e-learning, is a useful way of returning to learning without leaving the comfort of your own home. It is especially useful for people who have caring commitments or for those who are unable to leave the home for other reasons, such as mobility restrictions. It is also a useful way of returning to learning for those people who might be uncomfortable about entering an unfamiliar learning environment.

The Open University

Most Open University (OU) courses are run through distance learning, although summer schools and meetings are arranged. The OU uses 'multi-media' techniques which include textbooks, printed matter, television programmes, radio broadcasts and home computing. It is the largest university in the UK with over 200,000 students. Although two-thirds of the students are aged between 25 and 44, students can enter the university at the age of 18 or when they are much older. The Open University does not require specific entry qualifications which means that the courses are open to anyone who has the will and desire to study the course.

Most OU students study part-time and many students maintain full-time employment during their studies. Students have their own tutors and meet them and fellow students at study centres or residential schools. OU courses can lead to diplomas, degrees or higher degrees, and costs vary depending on the type of course and subject. A list of the different courses and subject areas can be obtained from their website or from the address below:

The Open University, Walton Hall, Milton Keynes MK7 6AA. Tel: (01908) 274066. www.open.ac.uk

Open University programmes are broadcast during the BBC Learning Zone, usually early in the morning. Anyone can watch the programmes which give an insight into what is taught through the OU. Details of the programmes to be shown can be found on Ceefax or by telephoning (0870) 900 9584. Alternatively, a *Learning Zone* magazine can be picked up from your local library.

The National Extension College

The National Extension College (NEC) is a non-profit-making trust dedicated to providing educational opportunities for all. The NEC provides distance learning courses in 140 subjects ranging from accountancy to writing and editing. Courses can be undertaken to obtain a qualification, as a first step on a new career, to improve your skills or for personal interest. Many students now study on-line, although printed study materials are provided for those without access to a computer. Personal tutor support is available via the telephone or e-mail.

You can enrol at any time of the year and work at a pace which suits you. It is also possible to decide whether or not you wish to take any examinations at the end of your course. The NEC tries to keep course fees as low as possible and will offer discounts to students who are on income support, unemployment benefit or state pension. Further advice on financing your studies can be obtained from the NEC's free *Guide to Courses*. To obtain a copy contact:

Student Services, The National Extension College, The Michael Young Centre, Purbeck Road, Cambridge CB2 2HN. Tel: (01223) 400350.

On their website you can order a copy of their course guide or browse an A-Z directory of courses: www.nec.ac.uk.

Learndirect

Learndirect offers 450 courses in subjects such as under-standing information technology and reading and writing skills. Courses can be studied at home if you have internet access or at a number of learndirect centres located around the country. All courses are studied on-line, so if you are not confident with using a computer you might be better visiting a centre where staff can help you with your work. Details of your local centres can be found in your local library or by consulting the learndirect website www.learndirect.co.uk. Alternatively you can ring the national help line for more information: (0800) 101 901.

There is a cost for the courses although vouchers may be available for some introductory sessions – ring the help line or check in your local library for more information.

SUMMARY

A useful way to think about the type of education available to you as an adult is in three sections – adult education, further education and higher education. Within each of these sections are various options, as the following list illustrates:

◆ **Adult education:**
    —access courses
    —university adult education departments
    —adult education service
    —adult residential colleges
    —Workers' Educational Association.

◆ **Further education:**
    —general FE
    —sixth form colleges
    —tertiary or community colleges
    —agricultural colleges
    —specialist colleges.

◆ **Higher education:**
    —universities
    —colleges of higher education.

In addition to attending a specific institution, adults may also consider distance learning or correspondence courses:

◆ **Distance learning:**
  —The Open University
  —The National Extension College
  —Learndirect.

FURTHER READING

For a comprehensive guide to further education consult the *CRAC Directory* which can be found in the reference section of your local library. The Careers Research and Advisory Centre produce this publication annually. It is a complete guide to over 75,000 FE courses in the UK, but also includes informative articles on further education and the qualifications that can be gained.

In the reference section of your local library you will find the *Springboard Which Degree Directory Series*. This is produced annually and covers all first degree courses available through UCAS. In 2002 the series was broken down into two volumes. Volume 1 covers arts, business, education, humanities, languages, law and social sciences. Volume 2 covers engineering, geography, mathematics, medicine, sciences and technology.

3

Understanding British Qualifications

Many adults find that when they consider returning to education, the qualifications available to them have changed so much since they were at school that they are unable to understand what they all mean. In this chapter a description of the most common British qualifications available for adults interested in returning to learning is provided.

However, some of the following qualifications, at first, seem to be very complicated. If you do not understand what some of them mean, speak to your tutor or an advice worker. Adults tend to find that when they begin returning to education, the mass of qualifications on offer become easier to understand, so please don't be put off or feel overwhelmed by this chapter – you will come to understand with time.

FURTHER EDUCATION QUALIFICATIONS

New A Levels (AS and A2)

Traditional A Levels have been replaced by a two-tier system and we are probably all familiar with the recent controversy this has created. Students study for the AS Level in the first year. Normally four subjects are chosen although some students will study five subjects. The AS Level is a qualification in its own right, so some students decide to finish their study after the first year. If students want to obtain the full A Level, they go on to study the A2 Level in the second year. Normally students are required to choose three subjects from the four studied in the previous year. The A2 Level, however, is not a qualification in its own right.

Vocational A Levels (AVCE)

This is the new name for the Advanced GNVQ. These qualifications are designed to offer more emphasis on vocational education and training, encouraging students to foster links with employers and work as part of a team. The AVCEs are available at three levels:

◆ 3 units = AS Level

◆ 6 units = 1 A Level

◆ 12 units = 2 A Levels.

At present AVCEs are offered in 14 subjects ranging from art and design to travel and tourism.

Scottish National Qualifications

Scottish qualifications have been reorganised recently and the changes should make it easier for adults returning to education. The new National Qualifications provide a broader range of options for progression from standard grade and are available at five different levels – Access, Intermediate 1, Intermediate 2, Higher and Advanced

Higher. The qualifications are made up of three units and each of these units (National Units) is a qualification in its own right. Students are able to build up National Qualifications and Units into Scottish Group Awards. These are larger qualifications built up unit by unit and can be equivalent to degrees, diplomas, HNDs, etc.

National Vocational Qualifications

These are work-related, competence based vocational qualifications. A list of competencies in a particular occupation is drawn up and a person has to demonstrate that they can meet the competence level required. Most NVQs are studied by people in full-time employment, although some can be studied at college with off-site training. There are five different levels of NVQ:

◆ NVQ level 1 = GCSE D/E grades

◆ NVQ level 2 = GCSE C grade

◆ NVQ level 3 = A Level

◆ NVQ level 4 = Degree/HND

◆ NVQ level 5 = postgraduate diploma/degree or professional qualification.

City and Guilds Qualifications

City and Guilds provide vocational awards in over 400 qualifications. They are designed to recognise skills used in the workplace and prove a person has practical skills in addition to theoretical knowledge. City and Guilds qualifications are available at a number of different levels in many occupations, ranging from catering to plumbing.

Access to Higher Education

Access courses are provided for people who wish to enter higher education through a route other than A Levels (see Chapter 2). Access courses can be studied full-time over one year, or part-time over two years. Successful completion of an access course leads to a 'kitemarked' award. The awards qualify students for entry into higher education.

National Open College Network

The National Open College Network (NOCN) was established in 1986. It is the UK's foremost provider of accreditation services for adult learning and is a major national qualification awarding body, offering qualifications from Entry Level to Level Three/Advanced in a wide range of subjects.

NOCN qualifications are designed with adults in mind and, in particular, are suitable for people who do not wish to follow traditional academic routes. Students are able to build up credits, accumulating and transferring the credits according to their needs. This means that you can study different courses at a variety of institutions if you wish. It also means that you can achieve qualifications in small steps over an amount of time that suits you. When enough credits have been accumulated, a full qualification is awarded. The credits are generally accepted as a means of entry to further study by further and higher education providers, and by a large number of employers and trainers. The accreditation service is designed to help learner motivation, achievement and progression.

The following list explains the level of credits on offer:

◆ Entry Level – measures individual progress, particularly in basic skills and self-confidence

◆ Level One – broadly comparable to NVQ Level 1, GNVQ Foundation and GCSE grades D to G

◆ Level Two – Broadly comparable to NVQ Level 2, GNVQ Intermediate and GCSE grades A to C

◆ Level Three – Broadly comparable to NVQ Level 3, GNVQ Advanced and A Levels.

Open College Networks (OCNs) are licensed by the NOCN. They are locally managed, not-for-profit partnerships committed to providing a flexible and responsive local accreditation service for a wide range of learning activities.

OCN partnership organisations include:

◆ adult and community education centres

◆ further education and sixth form colleges

◆ voluntary and community organisations

◆ universities and higher education institutions

◆ trades unions and employers

◆ local education authorities

◆ training organisations.

You can find out about Open College Network (OCN)

courses from your local college or from Learndirect (see Chapter 2). Or you can visit the NOCN website which contains a map and linked websites of all the OCNs in the UK. These provide detailed descriptions of available opportunities.

For further information, contact the NOCN:

National Open College Network, University of Derby, Kedleston Road, Derby DE22 1GB. www.nocn.org.uk

HIGHER EDUCATION QUALIFICATIONS

First Degrees

Most higher education courses lead to a First Degree. This could be a Bachelor of Arts (BA), a Bachelor of Science (BSc) or a Bachelor of Education (BEd). Most First Degree courses tend to run over three years for full-time study, although some full-time degree courses may run over four years, with one year for work or study placement. Degrees can also be taken part-time and may run for around five years. Some degrees are academic in nature, such as those in history or sociology, whereas others are more vocationally orientated, such as those in education or engineering.

In many higher education institutions subjects are now studied in **modules**. This means that students can study a variety of modules which make up their degree. In a standard year a student would need to complete 120 credits by studying a selection of modules, each worth anything from ten credits upwards. Some institutions, however, tend to follow a more traditional, single subject course, or specify the amount and type of modules that can be taken together.

First Degrees are classified in the following way:

◆ 1st (over 70% in exams and coursework)

◆ 2:1 (60 – 69%)

◆ 2:2 (50 – 59%)

◆ 3rd (40 – 49%)

◆ Fail (less than 40% in coursework and exams).

Higher National Diploma and Higher National Certificate

Higher National Diplomas (HNDs) tend to be studied full-time over two years and are advanced, vocational courses that relate to a particular occupation or field. The Higher National Certificate (HNC) is usually the part-time alternative to HNDs. Some students without the required entry qualifications for a full degree enrol on an HND course and then move on to a degree course.

Foundation Degree

Foundation Degrees are new, vocational, two-year courses that have been piloted recently. Eventually they will replace the HND. It is hoped that Foundation Degrees will provide an alternative route to higher education. These Foundation Degrees could suit adult learners, although it is too early to talk of their success.

Diploma/Certificate of Higher Education

These qualifications are offered by many higher education

institutions. The certificate is generally studied over one year full-time and the diploma usually takes two years of full-time study, although both can be studied part-time. Following the completion of a diploma or certificate in higher education, students gain credits which can be built up towards a degree course at a later stage.

POSTGRADUATE QUALIFICATIONS

Postgraduate Certificates and Diplomas

Postgraduate Certificates and Diplomas are studied over one year full-time, two-years part-time or through distance learning. The qualifications are available in a wide range of subjects and tend to be vocationally orientated. The certificate is at a lower level than the diploma. These qualifications are available as stand alone courses or can be part of a Master's course.

Postgraduate Certificate in Education

Postgraduate Certificates in Education (PGCEs) are available for people with a first degree who want to go into teaching. The courses are generally either one year full-time or two years part-time and students are required to carry out a good deal of classroom practice during their course.

Master's Degree

Masters' Degrees tend to be studied by people who have already received a first degree, although adults who are able to demonstrate a suitable level of work experience and competence may be admitted to a course without a first degree. Masters' Degrees are either taught for at least one year full-time or two years part-time, although some institutions will offer the courses through distance learning. Some Masters' courses are not taught courses but are **research** courses which mean that a student undertakes a piece of research, usually over two years.

Master of Business Administration

The Master of Business Administration (MBA) is a qualification for those people interested in management and business. People who are able to demonstrate the required level of experience and competence will be accepted onto a course without a first degree. Courses can be studied full-time over one year, part-time over two years or through distance learning. Part-time courses are becoming increasingly popular as people can combine the course with employment. Evening classes or distance learning also make studying for an MBA easier for employed adults.

Doctor of Philosophy

Studying for a postgraduate Doctorate involves in-depth research into a specific topic, decided upon by the student or institution. Entrants will need a first degree or a Master's Degree to be accepted on a doctorate programme. A student may conduct the research over a three or four year period full-time or over four to five years part-time, although some people take much longer to obtain their Doctorate.

New route PhD

Using this route a student can study for a Doctorate over a four-year period and combine a specific research project with a coherent programme of formal course work and professional skills development. At the moment only ten universities offer this qualification.

SUMMARY

A useful way to consider British qualifications is to look at further education level, higher education level and post-graduate level, as the following list illustrates:

◆ Further education qualifications:
  —new A Levels (AS and A2)
  —vocational A Levels (AVCE)
  —Scottish National Qualifications
  —National Vocational Qualifications
  —City and Guilds Qualifications
  —access to higher education
  —National Open College Network.

◆ Higher education qualifications:
  —First Degrees
  —Higher National Diploma and Higher National Certificate
  —Foundation Degree
  —Diploma/Certificate of Higher Education.

◆ Postgraduate qualifications:
  —Postgraduate Certificates and Diplomas
  —Postgraduate Certificate in Education
  —Master's Degree
  —Master of Business Administration
  —Doctor of Philosophy
  —New Route PhD.

4

Seeking Advice and Guidance

Advice about returning to education can come from many sources. When you obtain advice and guidance concerning your future learning, it is important to recognise the difference between **partial** and **impartial** advice. This is because some people offering advice might have other agendas, rather than your best interests at heart.

Broadly speaking, the type of advice and guidance you may receive can be divided into two categories – **informal** and **formal** advice.

INFORMAL ADVICE

As Chapter 1 has illustrated, there are many different reasons why adults decide to return to education. Often, these reasons will have an influence on the type of advice sought and received. For example, if you know that you are about to experience some significant life change, you might be open to receiving advice about returning to learning from many informal sources. You might have discussions with friends who've returned to education themselves; you might take note of short stories, films or television programmes that touch upon the subject.

All these sources of informal advice are valuable and useful. Talking to people from a similar background to you is very important. They can explain the returning process and their experiences from a personal point of view. It gives a human side – the pros and the cons; the high points and the low points; the good aspects and the bad aspects. They can give you invaluable pieces of advice that may not be considered to be significant by a professional. Also, they can help to dispel many of the myths or misconceptions you might have about what the adult education system is really like.

However, when you receive this type of informal advice, you need to recognise that it is not impartial. It is understandable that someone who has enjoyed a course will speak highly of that particular course and/or institution. But you must remember that it might not be the most appropriate course or institution for you. It is important to look at a variety of options so that you can make the most suitable choices for you. This is where formal advice is important.

FORMAL ADVICE

Today, there are many places where adults can seek formal information, advice and guidance, although the level, variety and standard differ throughout the UK. However, you need to recognise that although this type of advice is described as formal, it still may not be completely impartial, as the following example illustrates.

Donna (29)

One lunch time I decided to go to the local college and find out about courses because I thought it was about time I did something with my life. I was coming up to 30 and I thought if I didn't do it then, I never would. So I went to this enrolment session at the college which was near where I worked. I thought it would be good to go there because I would be able to go straight to the class from work. I had a bit of an idea what I wanted to do so I told the person at reception and she sent me to talk to the psychology tutor. I ended up enrolling on that course because the tutor seemed to suggest that was what I wanted. As the course progressed, I realised it wasn't psychology I was interested in but sociology. I'd not been given the option of talking to anyone else about what I really wanted to do and I think the psychology tutor was making sure he had enough people on the course. In the end I didn't mind the course; I just wish I'd had a bit more of a discussion with other people first.

In most institutions courses without the required number of students cannot run. This is why a minority of tutors may not be as impartial as we would like. However, many institutions employ experienced advice and guidance workers. If you live close to a college and feel that it would be the most convenient place at which to study, it is best to try to speak to the college advice and guidance worker as they will be able to help you make the right choices. Obviously they will be employed by the college and will tend to recommend courses run by the college, but if you have decided that this is the most convenient institution at which to study, then that is not a problem. Phone the institution in which you are interested and the receptionist will put you through to the right person to make an appointment.

However, if you are unsure of what and where to study, you need to speak to someone who knows about a wide variety of learning providers, courses, qualifications and subject areas, and who is able to match your learning with your ideas for the future.

When I was conducting some research into adults' learning choices I encountered an interesting phenomenon. In the same city some adults believed that there was no advice and guidance available to them, whereas others thought there was a lot of help available. Yet this was in the same city, where the same help was available to everyone. I asked the adults why this might be. Some felt that they were not very 'confident' at seeking out advice, whereas others believed themselves to be 'pushy', trying to get all the help they believed they deserved. For some adults, entering a careers centre that they perceived to be full of young people was quite intimidating, so much so that it almost rendered the centres invisible to them.

This made me realise the importance of listing different sources of information, advice and guidance – what suits one person may not suit another. Below I've listed four different ways of obtaining this advice in the hope that one or more of the methods will be of use to you.

GUIDANCE INTERVIEWS

Face-to-face interviews are usually the best way of obtaining personal, one-to-one information, advice and guidance. Every adult is different and an experienced adviser will be able to ask the right questions and offer the most appropriate advice.

The amount and level of advice and guidance offered to adults varies considerably throughout the UK. Some counties have much more developed services than others and if you are lucky enough to live within one of these counties you should be able to seek the appropriate information, advice and guidance without too much trouble. Look in the *Yellow Pages* under 'Adult Education Services'. If there is no entry under this topic try 'Careers Advice' and choose those that mention careers *and* learning opportunities in their advertisements.

Some careers advice centres, usually located within city and town centres, will have a walk-in service. You can discuss your needs with a trained adviser and if you need a longer interview one will be arranged for a convenient time. Some of these centres will have advisers trained to work with adults. Even if you are not interested in pursuing a career, they should be able to help you with your learning choices. However, check first that the careers centre does not make a charge for offering advice and guidance to adults. Some may offer an initial free interview and then charge for additional services. All people with disabilities, including adults, are entitled to free careers advice and guidance.

Connexions

Connexions is the new name given to centres that offer advice to young people. Although they may not be able to offer advice to adults, they will be able to point you in the right direction. For example, in my local area the Connexions advice shop is in the town centre on the High Street. In the window is placed a notice stating that adult guidance sessions will take place at the local Job Centre on Wednesday afternoons. My local area also runs a 'connect to learning network' which brings together local organisations to provide quality advice and support on learning and work issues for adults. A number of information points are located around the county and a free phone number is available. Adults are offered a free **learn and work check** which involves a 20-minute informal discussion with a trained adviser, either over the telephone or face-to-face. If you live in Dorset, this service is available for you. Contact the network coordinator for further information:

The Network Co-ordinator, Connect to Learning Network Centre, 3 Kingland Road, Poole BH15 1SH. Tel: (0800) 358 3888. www.dorset-careers.co.uk

If you live elsewhere in the UK, consult the *NIACE Yearbook* (details below) for details of your local 'information, advice and guidance network'. Also included in this book are addresses of regional learning guidance providers. Contact organisations in your area and find out what type and level of advice they provide for adults. You can also ring learndirect: (0800) 100 900 for details of your local IAG provider.

Unfortunately, however, in some areas of the UK you will find that there is very little face-to-face, impartial advice available to adults. If this is the case in your area, you may need to try one of the national help lines listed below or try the internet.

TELEPHONE HELP LINES

Telephone help lines are useful if you already have some idea of what you want to study, but need to find out where that type of course is available. Some of them might not be so good at offering the type of personal, tailor-made advice that is obtained in face-to-face interviews.

Learndirect (0800 100 900)

Learndirect was launched in 1998 and offers national learning advice via a free phone number or via its website (see below). The lines are open from 8am – 10pm seven days a week and the advice is free and impartial, covering over 500,000 courses nationwide. When I rang the number, I found it useful to have a fairly specific idea of what and where I wanted to study – the service was not so good for offering general advice about returning to learning. However, this might depend on the skill and experience of the person on the other end of the telephone – you could always try ringing again and speaking to someone else. The learndirect number for Scotland is (0808) 100 9000.

Local help lines

Some local careers centres will offer advice on the telephone. If you live a long way from the centre, ring to find out if this is the case, but check that the service is free for adults.

THE INTERNET

If you have access to the internet and feel confident using it, there are several organisations that offer advice and guidance on-line. Some of these offer general advice whereas others will offer advice tailor-made to your particular circumstances. However, you must remember that some of these services will use computer programmes to analyse the data you give – often there is no human involvement at all. This means that all those little signs about how you are feeling and what you are thinking that will be picked up by an experienced adviser, are missed by a computer. However, many people prefer the anonymity of this type of analysis, and if that is the case for you, this type of on-line advice might be the most appropriate method to use. Most services offering this type of advice now require you to pay a subscription fee.

Some national association websites do not offer specific advice to members of the public, but instead provide useful links to other organisations, as the following list illustrates.

www.prospects.ac.uk

If you already have an undergraduate degree, this website might be useful. It is the UK's official graduate careers website and contains advice and guidance about careers, jobs and further study. In particular it has a detailed list of the postgraduate study opportunities available which can be searched by subject, institution and/or region.

www.guidancecouncil.com

The Guidance Council is the national representative body for the sector. Although it does not provide advice and guidance directly to the public, it is a useful website for finding other relevant addresses and useful links. The site contains an interactive map which enables you to find out about local information, advice and guidance services.

www.careers-uk.com

The Careers Services National Association is an association of all the careers service organisations funded by the government. If you go to this website you will find a map of the UK – click on the region in which you are interested and all the names, addresses and telephone numbers of careers services in your area will appear. Most local services have their own website and some will offer advice and guidance over the internet. Check first whether there is a charge for this service.

www.ecctis.co.uk

UK Course Discover is an information database that provides quick and easy access to information on over 100,000 academic and vocational courses at universities and colleges throughout the UK. Users are able to view comprehensive details of course content, entry requirements, duration, type of course and qualifications awarded. However, if you access this site on your personal computer you will have to subscribe to the database. Some libraries and careers centre will have access to the database which is free to individuals.

Also included on this site (without the need to subscribe) is a detailed description of every university and college in the UK, including name and address, site map, number of students, cost of accommodation, cost of a pint of lager and a list of the clubs and societies. The site also gives a detailed list of British qualifications that can be obtained in further and higher education (see Chapter 3).

www.learndirect-advice.co.uk

Through this site you can access the learndirect course data-base which contains details of over 500,000 learning opportunities. If you have a specific query it is possible to e-mail one of the advisers. You can also access learndirect *futures* which is designed to help you think ahead about your future career. This is described as 'a unique internet based careers guidance and diagnostic software package' that allows you to learn more about yourself and your career preferences by matching your skills and interests to opportunities in the workplace. It offers advice on about 600 occupations, along with details about required qualifications and aptitudes. At the moment access to the database is free but in the near future there will be a subscription required. Also included on this site is access to the Job Centre Plus nationwide database which has details of over 300,000 vacancies in the UK.

In addition to these services are provided links to sites giving details about childcare provision in your area, funding for your studies, benefits, job fairs and help with special needs.

WRITTEN MATERIAL

Some people, especially when in the early stages of deciding what to study, prefer to collect written material, gathering information which they can digest at their leisure. If this is the case with you, there are a number of ways in which you can obtain information useful to the returning process.

Local libraries

Most local libraries will contain an education section in the reference department. This will hold books about universities and colleges, degree courses, institution prospectuses, sources of funding and so on.

Careers services

If you have a local careers centre it will contain leaflets and booklets about returning to learning. In most cases you do not need to make an appointment and will be able to take some leaflets away, although some material will be for reference only. You could try requesting some leaflets in writing, but be specific about what you require.

The Learning and Skills Council (LSC)

The LSC was established in April 2001, replacing the Training and Enterprise Councils and the Further Education Funding Council. The LSC intends to increase adult participation in learning and improve the quality and effectiveness of education and training. The LSC is divided into local councils which can offer information and advice about what is happening in your region. To find out the address and telephone of your local Learning and Skills Council contact:

Learning and Skills Council, Cheylesmore House, Quinton Road, Coventry CV1 2WT. General Enquiries Helpline Tel: (0870) 900 6800. www.lsc.gov.uk (this provides contact details for all local learning and skills councils).

The Department for Education and Skills (DfES)

The DfES provides information on many aspects of education and returning to learning. It has a comprehensive website that covers issues of student funding, mature students, part-time learners and so on. It also produces a number of booklets for prospective students. Write for more information or consult their website:

Department for Education and Skills, Sanctuary Buildings, Great Smith Street, London SW1P 3BT. www.dfes.gov.uk

SUMMARY

Advice and guidance can be divided into two categories – informal advice and formal advice, as the following list illustrates. It is important for adults to recognise the difference between impartial and less partial advice.

- Informal advice:
  - —friends
  - —family
  - —fellow students
  - —work colleagues.

- Formal advice:
  - —guidance interviews
  - —telephone help lines
  - —the internet
  - —written material:
    - local libraries
    - careers service

- Learning and Skills Council
- Department for Education and Skills.

USEFUL ADDRESSES

The Guidance Council, 2 Crown Walk, Jewry Street, Winchester SO23 8BB. Tel: (01962) 878340. www.guidancecouncil.com

This organisation is the national representative body for the guidance sector and, although not offering advice directly to the public, will provide names and addresses of guidance organisations in your area.

Women Returners' Network, Chelmsford College, Moulsham Street, Chelmsford, Essex CM2 0JQ. Tel: (01245) 263796. www.women-retuners.co.uk

This organisation provides information, advice and guidance to all women thinking about returning to education.

FURTHER READING

Edmunds, H.B. (ed.) (2002) *Directory of Guidance Provision for Adults in the UK 2002*, 7th edition, Kettering: ADSET.

Edmunds, H.B. (ed.) (2002) *Directory of Sources of Lifetime Learning and Career Development Information,* 9th edition, Kettering: ADSET.

NIACE (2001) *Adult Learning Yearbook 2001-2002: A Directory of Organisations and Resources in Adult Continuing Education and Training,* Leicester: NIACE.

5

The Financial Cost of Returning to Education

You may be worrying that returning to education will be too expensive and that the costs will exceed your income. Returning to education *can* be expensive, but it does not *have* to be expensive. With some careful planning and armed with all the necessary information, study can be cheap, if not free. In Chapter 6 all the ways in which you can obtain financial support to help with your studies are outlined. It is advisable to get hold of all the relevant leaflets or guides and study them in detail. You should make sure you get all the financial help to which you are entitled. After all, the money is there for people like you; why not make use of it?

However, before you go on to plan your sources of financial support, it is useful to start to think about what costs you are likely to incur when returning to learning. In my research, adults who had returned to education were asked to rank those things which they felt had been the most expensive. The list below itemises these costs, with the most expensive first.

> **Costs incurred**
>
> Course fees – 'tuition' fees, fees for course, examination fees
>
> Childcare – childminders, nursery places, babysitters
>
> Books
>
> Travel
>
> Photocopying/laser printing
>
> Food/drink
>
> Stationery – pens, paper, etc.

COURSE FEES

Course fees vary enormously, depending on the course you have chosen and the institution at which you wish to study.

Fees for private training

As a general rule private training providers tend to be the most expensive, although there will be exceptions to this rule. In particular, be wary of some information technology and computing courses run by private companies as the fees can be astronomical. If considering a course from a private training provider, find out exactly how much the course costs before you enrol. Make sure you look at the *whole* course and not just a specific module or component of the course.

Some less scrupulous learning providers are reluctant to detail fees up front. If this is the case, move on to another provider. If the course is vocational, that is it will help you with your future employment in some way, you might qualify for a Career Development Loan which will help with the cost of the course (see Chapter 6 and Appendix 2).

However, you will need to find out whether your chosen learning provider is registered with the DfES before you can apply for a CDL.

Tuition fees (higher education)

When you hear the term 'tuition fees' it generally means the fees you have to pay for a higher education, undergraduate course. On average, a higher education course will cost about £4,000, with most of this cost being met by the Government. However, now a student is required to contribute towards this cost and this is where 'tuition fees' come in. In 2002, the maximum amount of tuition fee a student has to pay is £1,100. Tuition fees are means tested – this means that many adults will only have to pay a part of the full amount and those on low incomes will pay nothing at all.

Fees for adult education courses and further education colleges

Most adult education and further education providers will give clear details of the fees for their courses, and most will accept payment in instalments – contact your local adult education service or FE college for details. Concessions are available on most courses, and those that do not attract concessions should be clearly marked. You need to check with your local adult education service and FE college, but as a general rule concessions are provided for the following:

◆ Those aged over 60 not in full-time employment.

◆ Those over the age of 18 who are receiving:
—Job-Seekers' Allowance

—Income Support

—Working Families Tax Credit

—Disability Working Allowance.

◆ For those under the age of 18 who are:
  —receiving Job Seekers' Allowance
  —on New Deal training courses
  —attending a college full-time and entitled to reduced fees.

◆ For students with a Statement of Special Educational Needs under the age of 19.

◆ In many colleges anyone not in the above categories can apply for remission of fees for any course on the grounds of financial hardship.

Examination fees

If your course is examined, you may need to pay an examination fee. Check with your learning provider as some examination fees are included in the cost of your course whereas others are not. Some students find it quite a shock to be asked to pay an extra examination fee at the end of their course. Concessions may be available for those on low incomes.

Refund of course fees

It is advisable to check with your learning provider whether they will give a refund on course fees should you be unable to attend. Most colleges and adult education services will give a refund up to around two weeks before the start of the course, but check specific time scales with your learning provider. Also, most colleges will provide a refund for any serious illness which prevents you from continuing with the course, but you will need to provide medical evidence that this is the case. You should also be aware that if you take out a Career Development Loan you will still have to repay the loan if you do not complete the course, even if this is not due to your own fault, such as the learning provider ceasing to trade. This means that you should be careful about the learning provider you choose.

CHILDCARE COSTS

If you have children you obviously have to think about how this might affect the cost of your course. Some parents wait until their children have entered full-time education before they consider returning to learning. This means that they do not have to pay for nurseries or childminders. Today there are a number of courses available aimed specifically at people with children. They are run during school hours and finish in good time for parents to collect their children from school (see Chapter 7). However, you will have to make sure that your learning provider and your children's school are not too far away from each other in order to keep down travel costs.

If your children are below school age you will need to find out about local nurseries or childminders. Telephone numbers may appear in your local telephone book or you might prefer to receive a recommendation from trusted friends. Some colleges have their own nurseries and concessions might be available – ring your local college to find out if this is the case. If you are on a low income, there are other ways of obtaining help with childcare costs or you might want to consider adult residential colleges which provide free places in their children's centres (see Chapter 7).

BOOKS

The number of books you will need to buy is dependent on your course subject, level and nature of the institution in which you are studying. On degree courses you will need to purchase some books as you will find that there will be too many people chasing too few books in the library. Textbooks can be very expensive and you need to make sure you have enough money available to cover these costs. However, costs can be reduced by buying second-hand books and by not buying every book recommended on the reading list (see Chapter 7).

TRAVEL COSTS

Obviously the closer the learning provider to your home, the less your travel costs. This is one reason why many adults choose to study close to home. However, adults find that there are sometimes unexpected travel costs, such as for fieldtrips or educational visits. When you find a course in which you are interested, speak to the tutor and find out whether there will be any extra travel costs for which you have to budget. Also, if you have children, make sure that your learning provider is close to their school so that you can cut down on travel expenses. There is financial help available for those on low incomes to help with travel (see Chapter 7).

PHOTOCOPYING/LASER PRINTING

Adults in my research pointed out that a 'hidden' cost, at least at the beginning of their course, was the price of photocopying and laser printing. The amount of photocopying and printing required depends upon your course, the equipment that you own and your preferred method of study. Some books needed for your assignments will be held only in the reference section of the library. This may be because the books are very popular or too big and expensive to loan to people. Some students photocopy the relevant sections which can be expensive. Costs can be kept down by taking notes instead of photocopying.

Many undergraduate courses require that you word process your assignments – if you do not possess a personal computer you will need to use a computer owned by the institution and most will charge for good quality print-outs. Some adults say that this can be very expensive – they've even found it cheaper to buy a second-hand computer. Colleges and universities make available student noticeboards and produce student newspapers in which cheap computers are advertised.

FOOD/DRINK

Young students who have just left home for the first time tend to find that most of their money goes on food and drink. However, as an adult you already understand the importance of budgeting – your know how to keep costs low where food and drink are concerned. Most colleges and universities have their own cafés, snack bars and restaurants, and, as a general rule, these tend to be slightly cheaper than those found on the high street. However, adults point out that costs can mount up. Most courses will contain a coffee break – you go to the coffee bar with your fellow students and buy a coffee. It is the sociable thing to do and much useful information is passed around during the coffee break. But do this twice a day, five days a week if you are on a full-time course, and costs mount up. Some adults take their own food and drink, whereas others do not buy a drink in every break. Some adult residential colleges provide free tea and coffee to help overcome this problem (see Chapter 2).

STATIONERY

Again, the amount of stationery you need to buy will depend upon your course. Pens and notepads are perhaps the most important items of stationery you will need and can be picked up cheaply from the college or university student union shop, or from the office warehouse shops which are open to the public. Some students find that buying in bulk from these places saves them money in the long run. However, it is advisable not to buy items of stationery until you have spoken to your tutor and found out exactly what is required. This could save you a lot of unnecessary expense.

SAVING MONEY

Adults were asked to provide their top tips for saving money when returning to learning. The following list has been reproduced from their answers, starting with the most popular.

Top ten money saving tips

1. Don't rush out and buy every book on the reading list. Buy second-hand books if possible.
2. Make sure you apply for all the money that is owing to you. Take up a free place in the nursery if you can.
3. Study in walking distance to your home. Bus fares and car-parking can be expensive.
4. Make your own sandwiches and have a plastic bottle which you fill with tap water or cordial.
5. Don't buy a large round of drinks in the bar – keep to small rounds or just buy your own drink; somebody will be glad you've suggested it. And don't offer to buy coffee for other people.
6. Don't bother photocopying pages and pages of books – you won't use all the information and it's a waste of paper and money. Take notes instead or just photocopy the really important points. Remember that some of the information is now available over the internet and it might be cheaper to print it from the internet rather than photocopy a hard copy of the book.
7. Ask your tutor for handouts – the tutor does not have to pay the cost of photocopying!
8. If you live a long way from the college, share the journey and cost with other students if possible.
9. Apply for college hardship funds and access funds – but you must be in real financial need.
10. If surfing the net, do it at college and not at home. Internet access is free for college students.

COPING WITH FINANCIAL PROBLEMS

If you find that your financial circumstances are causing you a great deal of concern, it is a good idea to seek advice. If you have already enrolled on a course, find out whether your college or university has a welfare rights officer. This person may be employed by the student services department of the college or university or by the students' union. As a student you are entitled to free, confidential advice and they will be able to let you know whether you qualify for any extra financial help.

If you have not enrolled on a course, contact your local Citizen's Advice Bureau for advice about the options available to you.

SUMMARY

It is important to find out about fees and expenditure before enrolling on a course so that you know how much your course of study will cost. This will save unexpected financial costs causing concern as your course progresses. The most common causes of expenditure for adults returning to education include:

◆ course fees – tuition fees, fees for courses, examination fees

◆ childcare – childminders, nursery places, babysitters

◆ books

◆ travel

◆ photocopying/laser printing

◆ food/drink

◆ stationery – pens, paper, etc.

When enrolling on a course it is useful to find out about fee refunds should you be unable to complete the course.

FURTHER READING

CRAC (2001) *Balancing Your Books 2001/02 – A guide to student finance,* Cambridge: CRAC.

6

Obtaining Financial Support

When obtaining financial support for your studies, there are several organisations you can try. However, your first enquiries should always be for government financial support. If you find that you do not qualify for this type of support, then you can try other organisations such as educational trusts and charities. These organisations will want to know that you have exhausted all forms of government funding before they are likely to offer you help.

The type of funding for which you can apply depends on whether you are intending to return to further education or higher education (see Chapter 2 for a description of each of these). It may also depend on whether you intend to study part-time and continue with your job.

GOVERNMENT FINANCIAL SUPPORT FOR FURTHER EDUCATION (ENGLAND AND WALES)

There are a number of funds available for adults who wish to study on a further education course. These courses may be either full-time or part-time:

◆ **College Access Funds** are available to help with additional costs such as transport, fees and books, although they are not supposed to cover living expenses. These funds are run by the colleges and are intended to help students of all ages. Funds tend to be allocated on the basis of need, with those in the most severe financial need receiving the most help. Funds are available once you have enrolled on a course. Contact your college welfare officer or student awards officer for more details.

◆ **Hardship Funds** are available for students facing serious financial difficulty, although not all colleges provide these funds. Talk to the college welfare officer or student awards officer once you have enrolled on your course. If these funds are not available, there may be other grants or bursaries available.

◆ **Educational trusts and charities** (see below).

◆ **Career Development Loans** (see below).

◆ The **Childcare Support Fund** is available to help with the cost of looking after your children while you are studying. If you are applying to a college, find out whether they have childcare funds available, although you may not be able to apply until you've actually enrolled. The funds mean that the college can offer free or subsidised childcare places at their own nurseries to lone parents or students on benefit or low incomes. Or they can help you pay for any other registered childcare provider, including nurseries, childminders and after school clubs. These funds are available if your children are under 15 or under 16 if they have a disability.

GOVERNMENT FINANCIAL SUPPORT FOR HIGHER EDUCATION (ENGLAND AND WALES)

For the purposes of financial support in higher education, the government distinguishes between **dependent** students and **independent** students (also referred to as mature students). In this chapter I will concentrate on independent students as most adults returning to education will be classified this way. However, if you are a young adult and dependent on your parents for financial support, contact the student support office of your Local Education Authority (LEA) for details about grants or consult the DfES website www.dfes.gov.uk/studentsupport.

Independent students are defined as:

◆ aged over 25

◆ or have been married before the start of the academic year for which they are applying for support

◆ or have supported themselves for at least three years

◆ or have no living parents.

In higher education the government will offer financial support for the following (all figures quoted refer to the year 2002):

◆ **Tuition fees** – most independent students will receive help with paying their tuitions fees. Many pay no tuition fees whatsoever.

◆ **Dependants' grant** – up to £2,480 for one child, more for each additional child.

- ◆ **Childcare grant** – up to £8,480 if you have two or more children.

- ◆ **School meals grant** – £225 for under 11s, £275 for over 11s, per child.

- ◆ **Travel, books and equipment grant** – £510.

- ◆ **Access bursary** – up to £500.

- ◆ **Hardship loan** – up to £500.

Information about all these grants can be obtained from the student support office of your local education authority. The telephone number will be in your local telephone book or can be obtained from www.dfes.gov.uk/studentsupport. Ask for an application form and a copy of the guide *Financial Support for Higher Education Students*. The guide can also be obtained by telephoning: (0800) 731 9133.

In addition to these grants, independent students may also apply for a **student loan**. In 2002 the amount of loan available was £3,905 outside London and £4,815 in London. The terms for repaying your loan are the same whether you are a full-time or part-time student. You will not have to start repaying your loan until the April after you have left or finished your course, and the amount you repay will be linked to your income. However, you will not have to make repayments while your income is below the threshold of £10,000 (2002 rates). You are not able to receive a student loan unless you have first applied for government financial support.

As soon as you have received an offer of a place at a higher education institution, you must apply for financial support (see Appendix 1). If you do not, you may be liable to pay your tuition fees which could amount to more than £1,100 a year.

Once you have taken up your place with your chosen learning provider, contact the student service or welfare department as soon as possible as some of the funds available to you will be administered by the institution rather than your LEA. For example, Access Funds and Hardship Funds will be administered by your university. You will need to apply once you have started your course and funds are given to those in the greatest financial need.

FINANCIAL SUPPORT FOR SCOTTISH HIGHER EDUCATION STUDENTS

In 2001/02 the Scottish Executive introduced non-repayable bursaries for both young and mature students who intend to enter full-time higher education, as well as an additional grant for lone parents with specific childcare needs. All students are also eligible to apply for Hardship Funds and Hardship Loans which are available through the institution at which you have been accepted.

In Scotland a 'young' student is defined as:

◆ not 25 or over on the first day of the first academic year of the course, or

◆ not married by the first day of the first academic year of the course, or

◆ has not been self-supporting through earnings or benefits for any three years prior to the first day of the first academic year of their course, or

◆ has no parent living but is under the age of 25 before the first day of the first academic year of their course.

If you do not fit into any of the categories above, you will be classed as a mature student and should consider a Mature Students' Bursary (see below). If you are a young student you may be eligible for a Young Students' Bursary of up to £2,050 (2002). The amount you get will depend on your family income and replaces part of your student loan.

The Mature Students' Bursary Fund is mainly available to help towards the costs of registered or formal childcare, particularly for lone parents. It may also be possible to apply for a payment to help with housing and travel costs. You apply for the funds through your institution and the amount you will receive will be based on your personal and financial circumstances. In 2001-2002 the highest payment a mature student could receive was £2,000.

Scottish students are eligible also to apply for student loans (see above) and Career Development Loans (see below).

Further details of the funding available for Scottish students can be obtained from:

The Student Awards Agency for Scotland, 3 Redheughs Rigg, South Gyle, Edinburgh EH12 9YT. www.student-support-saas.gov.uk

POSTGRADUATE FINANCIAL SUPPORT

If you are applying to study on a UK postgraduate course, that is a course which is considered to be above degree level (see Chapter 2), there are six research councils to which you can apply for funds. The following table details the names and addresses, value of funding and examples of the types of programme areas that are funded by each of these councils.

Contact the funding council or consult their website to find out whether you might be eligible for funding. However, as a general rule, to be eligible for a research council award you must be what is called 'ordinarily resident' in the UK throughout the three years preceding your application. You should also possess a first-class or upper second-class honours degree from a UK higher education institution, although there are exceptions to this rule. Nominations are usually submitted by the institution at which you have been offered a place.

Contact details	Value of grants (2002)	Example programme areas
Economic and Social Research Council (ESRC), Polaris House, North Star Avenue, Swindon SN2 1UJ. Tel: (01793) 413043. www.esrc.ac.uk	London £9,750 Outside London £8,000. Also pays: young dependants' allowance; disabled students' allowance; mature students's incentive	Economic and social history; human geography; management and business studies; linguistics; political science; psychology cognitive sciences; social policy, social work and health studies

Biotechnology and Biological Sciences Research Council (BBSRC), Polaris House, North Star Avenue, Swindon SN2 1UH. Tel: (01793) 413348. www.bbsrc.ac.uk	London £10,500 Outside London £8,500	Biomolecular sciences; biochemistry and cell biology; genes and developmental biology; animal sciences; plant and microbial sciences; engineering and biological systems; agrifood
Engineering and Physical Sciences Research Council (EPSRC), Polaris House, North Star Avenue, Swindon SN2 1ET. Tel: (01793) 444000. www.epsrc.ac.uk	Minimum stipend for all PhD students £7,500 Engineering Doctorate minimum stipend £9,000	Chemistry; engineering for infrastructure and the environment; engineering for manufacturing; general engineering; IT and computer sciences; materials; mathematics; physics
Medical Research Council (MRC), 20 Park Crescent, London W1N 4AL. Tel: (020) 7636 5422. www.mrc.ac.uk	London £12,500 Outside London £10,000	Medical

Particle Physics and Astronomy Research Council (PPARC), Polaris House, North Star Avenue, Swindon SN2 1SZ. Tel: (01793) 442118. www.pparc.ac.uk	London £9,700 Outside London £8,000	Particle physics, astronomy and astrophysics; solar system science
Natural Environment Research Council (NERC), Postgraduate Support Group Awards and Training, Polaris House, North Star Avenue, Swindon SN2 1EU. www.nerc.ac.uk	London £9,250 Outside London £7,500. Also pays: young dependents' allowance; disabled students' allowance; mature students' incentive	Earth observation; earth sciences; freshwater sciences; marine and atmospheric sciences; terrestrial sciences

More details of funding for postgraduate courses can be obtained from www.prospects.ac.uk.

FINANCIAL SUPPORT FOR TEACHER TRAINING

If you are applying for an undergraduate teacher training course, you are eligible to apply for a student loan and you will have your tuition fees paid. Even if you intend to study on a part-time course you are eligible to apply for a full-time student loan. If you intend to teach in one of the secondary shortage subjects you may be eligible to have your loan repaid for you. In 2002 the shortage subjects are:

- design and technology

- geography

- information technology

- mathematics

- modern foreign languages

- music

- religious education

- science.

In addition to having your loan repaid for you, it may be possible to qualify also for an additional hardship fund of up to £5,000 if studying in one of these shortage subjects.

If you intend to enter teaching via the postgraduate route, that is, you already have an undergraduate degree, you may be eligible for a training bursary of £6,000 which is not taxable.

Trainee teachers may also be able to apply for hardship funds or loans, help with childcare, travel and other course-related costs.

If you are aged 24 or over you may be interested in finding out about the Graduate Teacher Programme or the Registered Teacher Programme which offer employment based routes into the teaching profession. Grants are available to cover the cost of training and the trainee teacher is paid a wage by the LEA or school providing the training.

Further information about any of the above schemes can be obtained from the DfES Student Support free information line: (0800) 731 9133, or from the Teaching Information Line: (0845) 6000 991. Your Local Education Authority should also be able to provide you with information about student support and additional supplementary grants available to trainee teachers.

FINANCIAL SUPPORT FOR NHS COURSES

NHS bursaries are available for medical and dental students and for full-time and part-time students on health professional courses. The Department of Health booklet *Financial Help for Healthcare Students* explains NHS funding in more detail and can be obtained from:

Department of Health, PO Box 777, London SE1 6XH. Tel: (0845) 60 60 655. www.doh.gov.uk/hcsmain.htm

For enquiries concerning NHS financial support in England contact:

NHS Student Grants Unit, 22 Plymouth Road, Blackpool FY3 7JS. Tel: (01253) 655655.

For enquiries concerning NHS financial support in Wales contact:

NHS Wales Students Awards Unit, 2nd Floor, Golate House, 101 St Mary's Street, Cardiff CF10 1DX. Tel: (02920) 261495.

For enquiries concerning NHS financial support in Scotland contact:

The Student Awards Agency for Scotland, Gyle House, 3 Redheughs Rigg, South Gyle, Edinburgh EH12 9HH. Tel: (0131) 476 8212.

For enquiries concerning NHS financial support in Northern Ireland contact:

The Department of Learning, Training and Employment, Student Support Branch, 4th floor, Adelaide House, 39-49 Adelaide Street, Belfast BT2 8FD. Tel: (028) 902 577 77.

COMBINING LEARNING WITH PAID EMPLOYMENT

If you intend to study part-time whilst you continue with your paid employment, there are other ways you may be able to fund your studies.

◆ Career Development Loans (CDLs) are available to cover costs such as fees, books and travel. They can be used for any vocational course, including Open University courses and postgraduate qualifications (see below).

◆ Company sponsorship – if you think the course you wish to study will enhance the work that you do, you may be able to receive sponsorship from your company. Contact your human resources department for further details.

◆ If you are a member of a trade union, talk to your union's learning representative who may be able to offer advice on union-supported courses.

◆ If you are working but on a low or middle income, you may be able to claim a Working Families or Childcare Tax Credit which are part of the same scheme and designed to provide extra help with childcare. For more information pick up a leaflet from your local tax office, Inland Revenue Enquiry Centre or Benefits Agency Office. Leaflets are available also at www.inlandrevenue.gov.uk, or you can telephone the Tax Credits helpline on (0845) 609 5000.

CAREER DEVELOPMENT LOANS

If you want to study on a vocational course, that is, the course relates to your employment or your future employment prospects, you can apply for a Career Development Loan (CDL). The CDL programme is operated by the Department for Education and Skills in partnership with three high street banks: Barclays Bank, The Co-Operative Bank and The Royal Bank of Scotland. Clydesdale Bank withdrew from the scheme in October 2002.

CDLs can cover up to 80% of your course fees. However, if you have been out of work for more than three months the loans will cover all of your course fees. You can claim for living expenses only if your course is full-time.

If you want to apply for a CDL and you are claiming state

benefits you need to contact your Benefit Office as the loan could affect your entitlement to benefit.

Repayments for CDLs do not have to be made while you are learning. The Department for Education and Skills pays the interest on your loan while you are learning and for a month after your course finishes. You will then start to repay the loan in line with the agreement you have made with the bank.

If you wish to apply for a CDL, you need to do so in good time as decisions can take a while. Ring the Career Development Loan Information Line: (0800) 585 505, approach one of the three high street banks listed above or visit www.lifelonglearning.dfes.gov.uk/cdl/ for more information. For a step-by-step guide to applying for a CDL, see Appendix 2.

THE ADULT EDUCATION BURSARY SCHEME

In the UK there are eight colleges that specialise in providing long-term residential courses for adults (see Chapter 2). A bursary scheme has been set up for adults who enrol on a full-time course of at least a year in length at one of these colleges. Students need to have been offered a place on a certificate or diploma level course and have to be recommended for a bursary.

The colleges offer university type education for adults in a supportive environment within the areas of social sciences and liberal education. Examples of subjects that can be studied include local history, politics, sociology, English literature, media studies and information technology.

Grants are given to students to cover the tuition fees and provide students with a suitable amount of money on which to live for the year. Also a dependants' allowance is given for those who need extra financial support. For students with disabilities additional grants are available.

If you are interested in studying at one of these colleges and need to find out about the bursary scheme, you are advised to contact the college in which you are interested. Addresses and telephone numbers are listed below. If you require further, general information about the bursary scheme, you can contact:

Awards Officer, Adult Education Bursaries, c/o Ruskin College, Walton Street, Oxford OX1 2HE. Tel: (01865) 556360.

Adult residential colleges in the UK

Coleg Harlech, Harlech, Gwnedd LL46 2PU. Tel: (01766) 780363.

Co-operative College, Stanford Hall, Loughborough, Leicestershire LE12 5QR. Tel: (01509) 852333.

Fircroft College, 1018 Bristol Road, Selly Oak, Birmingham B29 6LH. Tel: (01214) 720116.

Hillcroft College (for women), South Bank, Surbiton, Surrey KT6 6DF. Tel: (020) 8399 2688.

Newbattle Abbey College, Dalkeith, Midlothian EH22 3LL. Tel: (0131) 633 1921.

Northern College, Wentworth Castle, Stainborough, Barnsley, South Yorkshire S75 3ET. Tel: (01226) 776000.

Palter College, Pullens Lane, Oxford OX3 0DT. Tel: (01865) 740500.

Ruskin College, Walton Street, Oxford OX1 2HE. Tel: (01865) 554331.

THE HELENA KENNEDY BURSARY SCHEME

The Helena Kennedy Bursary Scheme was launched in 1998. It is a registered educational charity and independent limited company established to encourage social inclusion and widening participation in further and higher education. It supports the 'second chance' education of individual students by awarding one-off annual bursaries of £1,000. The money is awarded as a 'contribution towards the direct costs of their commitment to lifelong learning'.

To apply, you need to be studying at a further education college at the time of your application and be intending to undertake a first time programme of higher education the following September. Only one application per institution will be considered.

For further details consult their website or contact:

Anne Faulkner, Helena Kennedy Bursary Scheme, c/o National Extension College, The Michael Young Centre, Purbeck Road, Cambridge CB2 2HN. www.hkbs.org.uk

EDUCATIONAL TRUSTS AND CHARITIES

In the UK there are a variety of educational trusts and charities that offer money in the form of bursaries, grants or loans to adults who wish to return to education. Names and addresses can be found in the *Educational Grants Directory* (details below) or from www.access-funds.co.uk.

If you decide to apply to an educational trust or charity you should first of all make sure that you have exhausted all sources of statutory funding. Trusts and charities will want to know that you have done this and will ask for details of any refusals. You should make sure also that the college to which you are applying does not have its own source of funding that could be offered to you.

When applying to trusts or charities ask only for an appropriate amount – find out how much the organisation usually offers and do not ask for more. You might stand a better chance of being successful in your request if you apply for the funding of something specific such as childcare or travel expenses.

Make sure that you do your research and apply only to the appropriate trust or charity. Many are very specific about what they will and will not fund – some specify age limits, whereas others will only provide funds for students from particular geographical locations or in specific areas of study. It is important not to waste your time filling in application forms which will be refused because you do not meet the funding criteria.

When you fill in an application form, tailor your application to suit the charity and make sure that you provide all the detail requested. Be honest and realistic – don't be too emotional or try to pull on their heartstrings. Write neatly, be concise and avoid jargon.

If you fail in one application, try another to increase your chances of being successful.

SPONSORSHIP AND BURSARIES

Some employers, especially of large organisations in both the public and private sectors, may provide sponsorship or training bursaries if the proposed course will help improve your work. Approach your human resources department for more details.

SUMMARY

When applying for financial support, you should always exhaust all forms of government financial support before trying other organisations. There are a number of funds available for adults, as the following list illustrates:

◆ Government financial support for further education (England and Wales)
  —College Access Funds
  —Hardship Funds
  —Career Development Loans
  —The Childcare Support Fund.

◆ Government financial support for higher education (England and Wales)
  —Tuition Fees
  —Dependants' Grant
  —Childcare Grant
  —School Meals Grant
  —Travel, Books and Equipment Grant

—Access Bursary
—Hardship Loan
—Student Loan.

◆ Financial support for Scottish higher education students
—Non-repayable Bursaries
—Career Development Loans
—Student Loans
—Hardship Funds/Loans
—Lone Parent Grant.

Other sources of financial support include:

◆ educational trusts and charities

◆ the adult education bursary scheme

◆ the Helena Kennedy Bursary Scheme

◆ company sponsorship

◆ research councils (postgraduate study).

USEFUL ADDRESSES AND WEBSITES

The Educational Grants Advisory Service is an independent advice agency for people who want to obtain funding for further or higher education. It is concerned mainly with providing advice for people who are not eligible for government funding, although it will provide advice on grants and loans if requested.

Educational Grants Advisory Service (EGAS), 501–505 Kingsland Road, Dalston, London E8 4AU. Information line – (020) 7254 6251 (open Mondays, Wednesdays, Fridays 10am–12pm and 2pm–4pm).

If you want to find out more about student loans, contact:

Student Loans Company Limited, 100 Bothwell Street, Glasgow G2 7JD. Tel: (0800) 405 010. www.slc.co.uk

Scholarship Search UK provides information about other sources of funding for undergraduate students. www.scholar-ship-search.org.uk.

FURTHER READING

CRAC (2002) *Student Support Sponsorship Funding Directory 2002,* Cambridge: Hobsons.

French, A., Griffiths, D., Traynor, T. and Wiggins, S. (2002) *The Educational Grants Directory 2002/3,* London: Directory of Social Change.

7

Overcoming Barriers to Learning

The term 'barriers to learning' refers to all those things that might get in your way and prevent you from returning to education. When adults were asked to discuss these 'barriers' the four most common were financial problems, lack of time, childcare responsibilities and negative perceptions and misconceptions. In this chapter each of these barriers is discussed along with possible ways to overcome them.

FINANCIAL PROBLEMS

Many adults say that lack of finance is the most restrictive barrier when returning to learning. It is true that some courses are very expensive and well beyond the financial means of most of us. If you find a course which is far too expensive, look for something else. There are so many courses available that you should find something more suited to your budget.

Adults also ask how they can justify spending so much when they are not sure of how the course will benefit them in the long term. Many adults find that if they cannot justify the expenditure to themselves then it is even harder to justify it to spouses or other members of the family, as Jane illustrates:

Jane (42)

I so desperately wanted to do the course. I've not really done anything for all my life, just bar work and cleaning and then I had the kids. But I do my husband's books and I know I could do book-keeping so I wanted to do the course. But it cost over £80 and money is very tight at the moment. If I did the course and spent all that money on me then the kids might have to go without something and I just don't think that's fair. But they're getting older and I don't want to be just a mum for all my life. I want to show people that I can do something, that I'm more than a mum. I was always good at maths at school and I could do the books of lots of people we know. But what if I didn't get the work, then I would have wasted the money and that's just not fair. So I just don't know. In a way I think it seems like I'm being selfish wanting to do this when I should be thinking more about the kids and my husband.

As a researcher on the outside of this family, it's easy for me to see that Jane is being far from selfish – she's constantly thinking about her husband and family, so much so that she is suppressing her own interests and desires in favour of theirs. Obviously there are many more issues involved in Jane's quotation, but at the moment we are concerned, like she is, with the financial issue.

Jane says that 'money is tight'. If, like Jane, you are on a low income, there are various courses that are free or offered at a lower rate:

◆ **Taster courses** or 'bite size' courses – check with your local college or adult education provider to find out whether they offer free short courses. These are designed for people who may not know exactly what they want to study, but who might want to try a few different courses without spending any money.

◆ **Concessions** – speak to staff at your chosen learning provider to find out what concessions are offered for people on low incomes (see Chapter 5).

◆ **Grants and bursaries** – there are various grants and bursaries available for people on low incomes (see Chapter 6).

◆ **Adult residential colleges** – through a bursary scheme places on courses at adult residential colleges are free. Meals, accommodation and childcare may also be free (see Chapter 6).

◆ **New Deal 25 plus** – this has been designed to help people who have been unemployed for at least 18 months. Under the Education and Training Opportunity scheme you can enrol on courses and learn new skills. Speak to your personal adviser at your Job Centre.

◆ **New Deal for lone parents** – with this programme you may be able to qualify for financial assistance for education and training, including childcare. Visit your local Job Centre or Citizen's Advice Bureau for more information.

For many employed people who wish to return to education, it is impossible, financially, for them to give up their full-time paid employment. If this is the case with you, there are still options open to you to help overcome financial barriers:

◆ Find out whether your employers will help finance you through your studies, for example, they might operate an employee development scheme through which money is administered for education and training. Some companies even arrange their own courses for employees.

◆ Look into obtaining a Career Development Loan (see Chapter 6 and Appendix 2).

◆ Choose courses that allow you to pay in instalments which will help you to spread the cost – ask your chosen learning provider for more information.

◆ Choose courses that allow you to study on a modular basis – you can take a module when you can afford it and build up your credits towards your final qualification. Ask your chosen learning provider for more information.

Financial barriers are often the most commonly discussed reason for people not returning to education. Often, however, 'lack of money' is an easily explained reason when really, as we can see in the above example from Jane, the reason is much more complex. She is battling with the *value* of education – will the long-term benefits outweigh the short-term expenditure? Can she justify spending money on herself when her children might have to go without? Will her children benefit if she completes the course? Will the whole family benefit?

There are many personal and family benefits to be gained by returning to education (see Chapter 10). When you are trying to justify the financial expenditure, think very carefully about these benefits. If you are still unsure about whether the long-term benefits will outweigh the short-term expenditure, try some free courses first, or speak to a friend or relative who has returned to education to gain an informed, personal opinion. This will help you to decide whether returning to education will be the right course of action for your personal circumstances.

LACK OF TIME

The next most common reason people give for not returning to learning is that they do not have the time available. Obviously, for some people this will be true. If you are rushed off your feet every minute of every day you will find it difficult to fit in some study time. However, if you really *want* to return to learning, you will *make* the time. Even so, you must be realistic about what you can achieve. If you have a very demanding job, for instance, you would not enrol on a course which takes up too much of your time and puts you under more pressure.

Today there are a wide variety of courses on offer which make it easier for us to fit learning in with our hectic lifestyles:

◆ **Distance learning, correspondence courses or e-learning** – these types of courses tend to be studied in your own time and at your own pace. You are not restricted to set hours and days of the week which is useful for anyone who has other demands on their time (see Chapter 2).

◆ **Part-time and short courses** – there are many different part-time and short courses available today to suit people from all walks of life. You might be interested in a morning class, an evening class or a Saturday class. Some courses may run for three days mid-week or over a weekend. Contact your local college or adult education service for more details.

◆ **Day release and block release** – you may be able to come to an arrangement with your employer which enables you to take off one day a week or one week every three months for a course. Some further education courses and postgraduate courses are designed with this in mind.

◆ **Study leave** – some understanding employers may provide a certain amount of time off for study, especially if the course will directly benefit your work.

◆ **Adult residential colleges** – some adults find that they do not have the time at home to study because there are so many people around them making demands on their time. Some people find it easier to move into college accommodation and study full-time, even taking their children with them (see Chapter 2).

If you think you do not have the time to return to learning, you need to sit and think carefully about this barrier. As Ned found, in the following example, 'lack of time' was actually another barrier, heavily disguised:

Ned (45)

I always used to say I hadn't got the time to go and do it. I knew I wanted to, but then I would look into it and say no, I just don't have the time. Also I think then the problem was that it was an evening class and it's so much harder to get motivated, when you've had a hard day at work, and you're sitting in front of the television, and it's raining outside, and you've got to go and sit in a classroom for three hours. So, although I said I hadn't got the time it was more than that really, I didn't actually want to do it enough. Then when I was threatened with redundancy I had all the motivation I needed. All of a sudden I had loads of time, even though really I had exactly the same time I'd always had. It was just I had a much stronger reason for doing it.

Ned is suggesting that if you have a strong enough reason for wanting to do something, time becomes available. However, if after careful consideration, you feel that you do not have enough time to enrol on a course, put the idea on hold for a while until more time becomes available. Returning to education should be an enjoyable experience and if it puts more pressure on you and causes greater stress, you are unlikely to stay the course or enjoy your experience.

CHILDCARE RESPONSIBILITIES

Having children should not restrict you from returning to learning. Members of the government have realised that many parents wish to return to education and they are introducing new schemes which should make the process easier. There are a number of ways in which you can fit learning around your childcare responsibilities, as the following list illustrates:

◆ **Learning during school hours** – many parents wait until their children are attending full-time education before they think about returning to learning. This means that they do not have to pay childcare costs. Today there is a wide variety of courses aimed specifically at women or parents. The courses are run during school hours and finish in time for parents to collect their children. Tutors are understanding and flexible if parents have to leave the course early if children are ill. Ring learndirect (0800 100 900) or your local college to find out whether there are any such courses run in your area.

◆ **Evening classes** – many parents register for an evening class so that their partners can look after the children, thus cutting down on childcare costs. However, you will have to make sure that your partner is happy with the arrangements so that further obstacles are not put in your way. Ring your local college or adult education service to find out what's available in your area.

◆ **Childcare Support Fund** – if you are on a low income you may be able to apply for financial support through the Childcare Support Fund (See Chapter 6).

◆ **Adult residential colleges** – some adult residential colleges have a limited number of childcare places available for students on their courses. College staff request that you try other sources first as the number of places is limited.

◆ **New Deal for lone parents** – with this programme you may be able to qualify for financial assistance for education and training, including childcare. Visit your local Job Centre or Citizen's Advice Bureau for more information.

◆ **Distance learning, correspondence courses or e-learning** – these courses enable you to study in your own time at your own pace. You can study at home if your children are able to occupy themselves or when they are at school or in bed (see Chapter 2).

However, as we have seen from Jane's example above, it is not just the practical issue of childcare, but also the emotional and psychological issues that are important to parents. They ask whether they are doing the right thing for their children. They are concerned about what might happen if their children are unexpectedly ill. They worry that other people might believe them to be bad parents, abandoning their children for their own selfish ends. Some of these concerns might seem over the top, but all have been aired on several occasions during my work with adult learners.

Children do benefit in a variety of ways from their parents returning to education (see Chapter 10). And many tutors understand the worries and concerns faced by parents – they will be flexible, enabling you to leave classes early if your children are ill. Some will let you keep a mobile telephone with you, as long as it is for emergency purposes only. Talk over any concerns you might have with your tutor, and don't worry what other people might think. You and your family almost certainly *will* benefit from you returning to education – that is what really matters.

NEGATIVE PERCEPTIONS AND MISCONCEPTIONS

I want to share with you some of the perceptions adults have had about education and the education system. Remember that all these are **negative perceptions or misconceptions** – in the second column I have attempted to dispel their fears.

Misconception	Dispelling the myth
They all walk around in gowns and funny hats up at the local university (Jim 41)	After three or four years of degree study students attend a graduation ceremony for which they hire or buy gowns and mortar boards. Only on graduation day will students wear these gowns, although there might be a few graduation days a year.
Young students are much cleverer than me. How will I be able to keep up? (Mavis, 53)	On average, mature students gain better grades than young students. Tutors report mature students are more enthusiastic and willing to learn.
University's for posh kids; it's not for the likes of me. (Dan, 29)	The élitist education system is changing, albeit gradually in some institutions. However, some of the newer universities are proud of their recruitment of people from educationally disadvantaged groups.

Nobody should be made to feel that they cannot succeed at university.

You can't teach old dogs new tricks. (Bert, 71)

We all learn every day of our lives. Anybody, any age, can benefit from returning to education. Some people believe that as we get older we might learn in different ways, but we still learn.

They'll all be young. I'll look so out of place. (Nancy, 58)

In the further education sector there are more mature students than 16–19 year old students. In many universities there are more mature students than 18–21 year olds. Some courses, however, attract younger students and some attract older students. Speak to the tutor if this is a real concern.

I'll be taking the place of a young person and they could benefit more than me. (Anne 39)

Places are not allocated on the basis of age. Everybody has the potential to benefit from a course, perhaps more so adult learners who have learnt the value of education and will demonstrate this through their enthusiasm.

I'll have to do an exam and there's no way I'm going to put myself through that. (Adam, 46)

Not all courses are examined – check the prospectus or speak to the tutor. Even qualification courses don't necessarily have examinations – they could be continually assessed, for example.

I'm so nervous. No one else can be feeling like me! (Joan, 31)

Almost everybody will be feeling nervous or apprehensive, but, like you, they will be trying to hide it.

Negative perceptions and misconceptions can lead to fear and anxiety. It is understandable that we should be anxious about something which is unfamiliar to us. This is why it is important to make something more familiar so that we do not waste time and energy fearing the unknown. There are several ways in which you can become more familiar with the education system and your chosen learning provider. These methods should help you to overcome your fears and anxieties:

◆ Many colleges and universities run open days or fairs where you can go and have a look around. Try to get a friend or relative to go with you so that you are not alone if you are nervous.

◆ Some courses, especially those run by adult education colleges, are aimed at adults who are nervous or anxious. They enable you to get together with other people and tutors in a supportive environment. Some will enable you to try taster courses so that you can see whether you can adjust to a learning environment.

◆ Talk to friends and relatives who have been through further and higher education. Their opinion is very important – it will give you a personal insight into learning which won't be available in institution brochures. You will soon find that most adult education is nothing like your experiences of school.

◆ Some tutors will arrange a social gathering before the course begins so that you can meet other students and start to dispel some of the misconceptions you may have.

Remember that everyone else is probably feeling the same as you. Even the young students are nervous – many of them have never been away from home before, or may just have left a sheltered school environment. Tutors understand your anxieties and will quickly help you to feel relaxed and comfortable.

Overcoming barriers to learning can be a hard thing to do, but if you really want to return to education, persevere. As Jamie found, it is worth it in the long run:

Jamie (29)
I'd been working in a factory for years, doing the same old mundane job over and over and over again. It was driving me crazy. I started to think about doing a course but I thought I'd never be able to afford it. I looked into some of these courses what come through the post. I couldn't believe the cost – some wanted about 200 quid. I get my wages on a Friday and they're gone by the following Wednesday. How could I fork out that? Then a mate went to the college and they said he didn't earn a lot so he could do the course for three quid! Three quid! I couldn't believe it. So I went and it were true. I got on a course and I got a really good pass. Then I went on another one and I got another good pass. My tutor said I were really good. Next year I'm packing it all in and going to university. God knows what I'll be doing after but I won't be working in that factory no more. Or maybe I will go back and be the boss!

SUMMARY

The most common barriers to learning faced by adults are:

◆ financial problems

◆ lack of time

◆ childcare responsibilities

◆ negative perceptions and misconceptions.

Financial problems can be overcome by making sure that you apply for all the financial help available to you. It is useful also to enrol on free courses until you get a feel for whether you would like to study further and pay a fee.

Today there are a wide variety of courses and learning providers on offer that make it easier for us to fit learning in with our hectic lifestyles:

◆ distance learning, correspondence courses or e-learning

◆ part-time and short courses

◆ day release and block release

◆ study leave

◆ courses at adult residential colleges.

Having children should not restrict you from returning to learning. There are a number of ways in which you can fit learning around your childcare responsibilities:

◆ learning during school hours

- evening classes

- Childcare Support Fund

- children's centres at adult residential colleges

- New Deal for lone parents

- distance learning, correspondence courses or e-learning.

There are several ways in which you can become more familiar with the education system and chosen learning providers to help overcome negative perceptions and misconceptions:

- Attend open days or fairs where you can go and have a look around.

- Attend a course aimed specifically at adults.

- Talk to friends and relatives who have been through further and higher education.

- Attend social gatherings before the course begins.

8

Coping with Change

Many of us have seen the film *Educating Rita*. Julie Walters goes away to university and begins to change, so much so that family relationships and existing friendships begin to break down.

You may be worrying that this might happen to you. This is understandable as, for some adults, returning to education is a major life decision which can cause considerable change. However, I must stress that thousands of people return to education every year and still remain happy with their wives and husbands, partners and friends. They find education an enriching experience which serves to enhance and strengthen existing relationships rather than cause ructions and disharmony (see Chapter 10).

The amount of influence returning to education has on existing relationships depends on a number of factors. Firstly, it will depend on the amount and type of education – if an adult is attending a yoga evening class once a week, there may be little effect, apart from that person becoming a little calmer mentally and more supple physically. But if an adult is attending a full-time degree course at a local university, obviously they are open to many more influences, from other students, staff and the whole process of studying. It is inevitable that there will be some change.

Also, the amount of change experienced will depend upon the reasons for returning to education. Some people return to learning because they feel they are stuck in a rut – they are unhappy at home or at work. Education is seen to be a means by which they can escape their present, unhappy circumstances. If this is the case, then changes are both expected and desirable. Obviously the problems arise if the adult returning to education has failed to mention, and discuss these issues, with those people close to them.

NEGATIVE AND POSITIVE CHANGE

In my research, adults were asked to discuss any changes they had experienced as a result of returning to education. They were asked to divide these into what they perceived to be 'negative' changes and 'positive' changes. As you can see from the following list, there are many more positive changes than negative.

Negative	Positive
Have become more argumentative with my partner when he doesn't support me	Become cleverer, more intellectual
Can't tolerate racism in my local pub	Can think clearer and more analytically

Have become a bit
boring to my friends,
so I'm told

No longer have cobwebs in my brain

Can understand intellectual discussions

Read 'proper' newspapers

Have made new and different friends

Feel more confident

Have become better at socialising

Am no longer shy

Can stand up for myself

Am no longer scared of what I don't
understand

Like taking part in new and different
activities

Horizons have been broadened

Found a new partner!

Self-esteem has gone sky high

Stopped smoking

Have become more tolerant

Can answer questions on University
Challenge

When compiling this list, adults had to think very carefully about whether a change was positive or negative. For example, several people said that they had begun to understand the issues surrounding racism and when they heard racist comments from their friends, they became very uncomfortable. Some would challenge the comment which would cause friction with their friends. They felt that this was a negative change in the sense that it caused problems with existing friendships, but all agreed that it was a good thing that they had become more aware of racism.

All the adults who took part in the research felt that it had been a really useful exercise to think about what changes had taken place since they had returned to education. They felt that this had been a useful way to cope with change, especially as it had reminded them that most change had been positive.

Many of the changes mentioned in the table above relate also to the 'benefits' to be gained and will be discussed in more depth in Chapter 10.

MAINTAINING EXISTING RELATIONSHIPS

If you are in a relationship with another person, and you wish to remain that way, it is common sense to discuss, and try to reach an agreement, on any decisions that will affect both of you.

At first, those close to you may be suspicious of your reasons for returning to learning. They may be feeling insecure, or they may feel that you are trying to move on without them.

By discussing your reasons for returning to education and talking about possible learning choices together, many of these problems can be overcome from the start.

Some adults cope with this type of change by enrolling on a course together so that they can support each other and experience change together. However, this may not be a practical solution for many couples as people might have different demands on their time.

Other adults find it useful to discuss any problems they are facing with other people who have been through the same situation. By speaking to students on their course, and to friends who have returned to education, adults find that they are able to understand that many people encounter the same problems and are able to overcome them.

If, however, you are aware that the problems are escalating and you are finding it difficult to cope, many colleges and universities have welfare and counselling services. By speaking to a professional you may be able to sort out the problems you are facing. All advice is free to students and the counsellor should have experience of dealing with this type of problem. Ask your tutor or consult your student handbook for more details of the services available.

I must stress, however, that these sorts of serious problems only occur on rare occasions. It is true that some couples may split up, but this is because there were more serious underlying problems present in the relationship in the first place. Returning to education may have helped to bring these problems to the surface, but will not be a sole cause of the problems, as the following example illustrates:

Michelle (35)

When I first said I was going to do a class Wayne started to take the micky. He said he was going out to buy me a pencil case and a satchel. Then he said he would get me a sexy school uniform. He just didn't take me seriously at all. I didn't say much because I was nervous about going back. I wasn't sure I could do it and I didn't want to make a big fuss in case I couldn't do it or couldn't pass the exam. Anyway, I did the O Level in a year and I passed with an 'A'. I was so surprised and really, really pleased, but all Wayne could say was oh, big deal, it's only an O Level, who wants those anyway?

So my tutor asked if I was going on to do the A Level and I thought why not? So I enrolled on that and I was doing really well. Then Wayne started to get funny about me going. He would drop me off and be waiting for me when I got out. He wouldn't let me go to the pub with the other students. I wasn't allowed to go to the Christmas party. Then he'd say things like I wasn't a good mother because if my kids were ill I wouldn't be at home for them. I said he was their dad and he could look after them like me, but he said that was my job. Before, I would have believed him and just shut up for a quiet life. But I didn't shut up this time. We had a huge row. He made me feel so guilty. I decided to pack the course in. But when I spoke to my tutor she asked if I really wanted to stop and I said of course not. So I decided to carry on.

Wayne just got worse and worse. In the end he would sit outside the classroom for three whole hours. Sometimes I would see him looking through the window to see what was going on. It began to get really scary. Anyway, the exam came and I passed and I got an 'A' again! Then I heard about an access course and thought I would do that. But Wayne just said no, if I did it he would leave me. I realised I didn't love him anyway; in fact I almost began to hate him. I would never stop him doing what he wanted to do, why was he stopping me? I'd not been allowed to be myself for years. He'd stopped me seeing my friends, he'd made me stay in the house, but I'd gone along with it because I'd thought that's what a wife was supposed to do. I'd been so unhappy for years and then when I finally was doing something I liked he tried to stop that as well.

We've split up now and it was the best thing I've ever done. I did my access course and I'm off to university next year. My children have really perked up as well. I hadn't realised how much their lives had been run by him. I think going to college and mixing with other people helped me to realise what I was missing. I've not looked back at all. It was the best thing I've ever done.

CLASS CONFLICT

Britain is a class society – sometimes people who return to education are accused, by their friends, of betraying their class. Again this happened in *Educating Rita* – she started to dress differently, cut her hair differently, took part in different social activities. Some adults describe this as a 'push/pull' feeling. On the one hand they are being pushed away from their friends who think that they are becoming 'snobby'; on the other hand they feel themselves being pulled towards people who have similar interests in the classroom.

For some adults this is a difficult time, as the following example illustrates.

Sally (29)

I knew someone who I'd known in drug rehab. She was doing an access course and all me mates were saying, oh, you don't want to mix with her; she's gone all snooty, you know what I mean? Well, it made me think well I'd better not go on the course 'cos they'll say the same about me. Then my social worker really pushed me and I thought ok, I'd give it a go. And they did try to stop me, some of them, they said I'd change. But others were really supportive and I knew I had to get out of the trouble I were in, so in the end I went for it. I've still got some of those friends which is good and now I've made loads more which is even better. My social worker were right. I'm glad I did it.

Sally was able to come through the difficult time because she realised that she still had the support of good friends and that she was able to make new friends as she progressed on her course. This is what many adults in similar circumstances find – true friends will support you. Ok, they might make jokes at the beginning, but if they see it is something you are really keen on, they will support you as much as you need.

Some adults suggest that if friends continue to put obstacles in your way, then perhaps they are not as good friends as you thought, and that maybe you should consider moving on to new pastures. Sally felt that, although some of her friends thought that she was becoming 'snooty' and perhaps moving between social classes, this was not really the case. Instead she felt that she was widening her social circles and beginning to understand more about herself. This was helping to reinforce the importance of her social and cultural roots.

EMPOWERMENT

Many adults report an increasing sense of empowerment as they successfully pass through the education system. Suddenly they are able to make sense of their lives and realise that they are able to take more control over what happens to them. At first, this can be a difficult situation with which to cope. Like Michelle, women (and men) can find that they are not happy with their lives and present roles, realising that they are not allowed to be themselves or reach their full potential. This can lead to arguments, tension and unhappiness with loved ones or friends, as Steve illustrates.

Steve (41)

When I started my university course I used to go to the local pub on a Saturday night and meet up with me mates. I'd done this all my life and I didn't want to change just because I was at university. But me mates used to joke about me supping me wife's money because she was working while I was studying. They said I was mad, why was I doing it when I could be down the building site grafting and earning. I said that's why I was doing it, 'cos I wasn't going to spend the rest of my life working bloody hard for a pittance. Then they'd start turning their noses up and going, oh, listen to him, he's too good for us. I tried to show how they could get out of it and do something more and get jobs that were better paid for much less work. They thought I was insulting them. Then they'd start on about people from other countries taking their jobs and I'd try and talk to them about how attitudes like that are what keeps them in the position they're in. That it's classic divide and conquer, keep people quiet by making them moan about something else other than what bad lives they've got. But they wouldn't listen; they'd just get annoyed with me or make jokes.

It was really frustrating and I found it affecting my relationships with them. I suddenly realised I was moving on in my ideas and they weren't. I had loads of sleepless nights trying to decide what I should do. In the end I realised I didn't want to lose some of those friends because where I come from is so important to me. So I have to try and keep a bit quiet when I'm with them. But I can see they're being kept down, they could do so much if they wanted. It's so weird when you can see what's happening to you and your mates, but nobody wants to listen or change their lives. But I know that anything to get me out of grafting's gotta be good.

Some tutors find it hard when they see their students going through such turmoil. However, it is only right that once people realise that they are not happy, they take steps to improve their lives. Some adults who return to education find that once they are able to gain access to more knowledge and information, they are able to challenge and change those aspects of their lives with which they are un-happy. Like Michelle, they come to realise that they shouldn't, and don't have to, put up with this type of unhappiness. In the short-term this may cause friction, but all agree that life is much better in the long-term after they have made the changes.

INTELLECTUAL DEVELOPMENT

Closely connected to the theme of empowerment is the issue of intellectual development. In the above example Steve shows how he found it hard to communicate with previous friends when they had not developed their thinking in a similar way. He still wanted to keep his friends and so had to keep quiet on issues that he felt would cause arguments.

All adults find that intellectual development is an expected and realised benefit of returning to education (see Chapter 10). However, what some do not expect is that this change can cause conflict in existing relationships. How you deal with this has to be your own decision – Steve felt that he would keep quiet, others have decided to 'move on' from friends who will not accept the changes, as the following example illustrates:

Jackie (24)

What brought it home to me was when I went for a night out with the girls. The conversation all night was about make-up, clothes and dieting. Don't get me wrong, before I'd gone to college I'd be joining in with the rest of them, probably more so where clothes were concerned. But this night I just listened to them and I thought it's not me anymore. I want to talk about more than that. I want to do more than that. I want to think more than that.

At college we'd looked at how advertising entices people in and here were my friends showing all the signs we'd talked about. It was as though I'd suddenly got loads more insight and they hadn't. Since I've been at college I've made more friends and we talk about so many different things, you know, quite often have intellectual conversations. I don't want to sound big-headed or anything, but it was just so much more fun. I've decided I'm going to move on from my old friends. Obviously I'll see them if they really want me to, but I don't think they will because I think they can see I'm changing as well. I don't mind not seeing them so much because as I say, I've met so many new people and I know I've changed.

Although you will have to decide how to deal with this issue, if you are aware that it can happen, you will be much better equipped to cope with problems should they arise.

TIPS FOR COPING WITH CHANGE

Adults were asked to give their tips for coping with change. These appear in the following list, with the most popular pieces of advice appearing first.

Tips for coping with change

1. Look upon every change, however small, as something positive.

2. Be open and honest with your partner – discuss change as it can scare people who don't understand why it's happening.

3. Don't change because you feel you have to – some people don't change at all.

4. Don't try to be something you're not, just because you think it's expected of you.

5. Don't talk too much about your course to people who are not interested. Save your intellectual discussion for people who share your enthusiasm! Your friends will thank you for it.

6. Don't try to convert people to your way of thinking if they're not interested – you will get a reputation for being a bore.

7. Understand that you might have to play different roles with different people.

8. Enrol on a course with your partner or a friend, then you both experience change together and you can support each other.

9. Don't waste time thinking and worrying about how you might change. You will soon find that it is not that important in the great scheme of things.

10. Get support from other people who have experienced what you are experiencing. We all experience some form of change throughout our lives. It's part of the human growth process and should not be feared.

SUMMARY

Most adults find that they change in some way as a result of returning to education. For some adults this change is very small and in some cases almost imperceptible – for others it is monumental. Although changes can be either positive or negative, most adults find that the change is positive.

The main areas of change occur in:

◆ existing relationships

◆ perceived movement between social classes, either from the adults themselves or from friends and relatives.

This may be due to:

◆ increased empowerment

◆ intellectual development.

9

Staying the Course?

The title of this chapter has been written as a question. The reason for this is that adults often believe they should persevere with an unsuitable course because it is expected of them or because other people would consider them to be a failure if they left. However, this should not be the case. If a course is not meeting your requirements, you should not feel compelled to stay. There are many other courses around which might be better for you. As an adult you should be happy with your learning – it should be an enjoyable and fulfilling experience. If it is not, you have the option to leave and try something else.

For many adults enrolling on a course is a gamble – they are unfamiliar with the education system and do not know what to expect. It is hard to know whether a course will be suitable for your needs until you have tried a few classes. Only then will you know whether it is really what you require. If, after this time, you find that it is not suitable, you should do something about it so that you are not unhappy with your learning.

There are many reasons why a course may be unsuitable, and, as you will see in the following discussion, these reasons are not due to any personal failure on your part.

UNSUITABLE TEACHING METHODS

We all learn in different ways. Some people prefer to work in a team, learning from each other through discussion, whereas others prefer to work on their own, using written sources. Some would rather use experimentation, trying different ways of solving a problem until they are successful. Others prefer to be told facts and commit them to memory.

Over the years researchers have spent a great deal of time trying to understand different learning styles. Some people believe that the learning style you were born with remains the same throughout your life, whereas others believe learning styles can and will change as you grow older. Today, on the internet, there are a variety of surveys which will help you to start thinking about your preferred learning style. Just type in 'Learning Style Survey' and see what comes up. I have tested two of these surveys and I would say that both are fairly accurate in terms of my learning style. Have a go at filling them in – it is an interesting exercise as it makes you think about the ways in which you retain information. However, you should always remember that this type of on-line survey can be open to misinterpretation and error. Therefore don't take the results too seriously.

An awareness of your learning style may help to point you in the direction of the right course and could help to overcome problems you might experience due to a mismatch in teaching and learning styles. However, good tutors will recognise that people learn in different ways and they will tailor their teaching methods to the learning style and preferences of people in their class. If they do not do this, students will not enjoy their learning, finding it an unfulfilling and dissatisfying experience. Often, older students perceive this to be a problem with their personal ability to learn, thinking that their brains are getting 'woolly' due to their age. However, you need to recognise that this is not the case. Instead, problems such as this are more likely to do with the *teaching style of the tutor* and not to do with the student's ability to learn, as the following example illustrates:

Ed (36)

I enrolled on a history course at my local college. I was really interested in history and thought it would be a good way back into education, so I started with the O Level and thought I would work my way up, maybe finally even doing a degree. Anyway, I enrolled on the course and I couldn't believe it. All the tutor did every week was write reams and reams on the blackboard and we had to copy it down. That was it.

He had notes he copied and probably had done since the year dot. We were expected to copy it all down with no discussion or anything. I found it the most boring thing I'd ever done. And I found it impossible to retain the information. At first I thought it was 'cos I was getting older, my brain had given up, but it was only when I started talking to another student that she said she couldn't remember anything that we started to question how we were being taught. I could only stick the course for five weeks. Then I left.

Later I went on a local history evening class and it was so different. We were given projects and we had to go out and about in groups. Find things and then work out their history. It was brilliant and I learnt so much. I can't believe the two courses could be so different.

UNSUITABLE SUBJECTS

Some adults find that they have enrolled on a course which is not what they expected. This is often because they have received inappropriate advice and guidance, as we can see from Donna's example in Chapter 4. There are hundreds of subjects available, offered by a wide variety of institutions. If you find that you are studying something which you really do not enjoy, you should not persevere if you do not wish to do so.

However, some adults who had decided to persevere found that they had enjoyed studying that subject, even though initial perceptions had been negative. It is useful to set yourself a deadline, and if your interest in the subject has not grown by then, you can think about studying something else. Some institutions will let you change to another course within a certain timescale – speak to your tutor as soon as you feel that you are unhappy to find out whether this is the case and, if so, the timescale in which you must make the transfer.

Most learning providers will not offer a refund on course fees if you leave due to lack of interest in the subject.

However, if you have enrolled as a result of inappropriate advice from someone within that institution, you may have a legitimate grievance that you wish to fight. Find out whether your institution has a student's union and speak to the education officer or welfare officer. This person will be able to help you build a case and represent you in a tribunal if you really are unhappy.

UNSUITABLE CLASSMATES

Some adults find that they have enrolled on a course which is full of people who are so different to themselves that they find it very difficult to learn. Adults describe their classmates in a variety of ways, giving the following examples as problems that have been encountered on some courses.

Unsuitable classmates: some examples

Most people were on day release from work. They treated the course as a means to escape work for the day. They were not interested in their learning, but would mess about, going to the pub at lunch time and coming back to the course drunk and boisterous. The tutor had a terrible time getting them to do anything and it was really distracting for us. (Louise, 24)

The youngsters wouldn't take the course seriously. There was even a culture of doing badly – it seemed to be trendy not to do the work or hand it in on time. Anyone who did was laughed at and considered a swot. The whole situation was quite uncomfortable. (Matthew, 37)

Other people on the course hadn't any family commitments. When we had project work to complete they would meet up in the evening at a pub, or on a weekend. They couldn't understand why that was impossible for me. (Adrianna, 32)

Others on the course were so posh. We had absolutely nothing in common. They would talk about their problems – their cleaner hadn't turn up on time or something like that, and I would think that's not really as important as not having enough money to put a meal on the table. They couldn't understand why I didn't go for coffee and dinner with them because I couldn't afford it. (Tiffany, 27)

In some cases adults are able to work around this problem, utilising the experience as a learning process in itself, especially if they have encountered people on their course who are from quite different social and cultural backgrounds. However, other adults have felt that the situation makes it impossible for them to learn, and have decided to leave the course in order to find something more suitable.

Always try to speak to your tutor before you enrol on a course to find out at whom the course is aimed. This should give you a good idea of the make-up of the class. If you feel you would be unhappy in such a class, think about looking elsewhere.

UNSUITABLE WORK-LOAD

As an adult returning to education you will probably have many more demands on your time than a school-leaver who does not have family commitments. Tutors should remember this also and courses for adults need to be designed with this in mind. However, one of the important parts of formal learning is that you develop time-management skills, personal organisation skills and self-discipline. Deadlines need to be set and met to help you develop these skills. Some tutors and colleges will be very rigid on these deadlines, only allowing extensions on work in exceptional circumstances. Others, however, will be much more flexible and understanding, providing longer deadlines or allowing extensions for adults with other urgent demands on their time.

Unfortunately, some course prospectuses fail to tell you about the work-commitment expected of you. If this is the case, try to speak to the course tutor before the start of the course. Most courses aimed specifically at adults should give you a general idea of what work is required when you receive information about the course.

Some adults find that family circumstances change as the course progresses. Initially you might find that you have plenty of time to do the work and are getting very good grades, but something happens in your family life to make it almost impossible for you to continue completing the work. If this is the case, talk to your tutor – there may be provision for this type of situation. Or you may be able to postpone your course and continue once you have more time available. This should not be seen as failure, but as a temporary adjustment in life and study.

LIFE CHANGES

Some adults find that, due to life changes beyond their personal control, it is almost impossible to continue with the course. As I have mentioned, learning should be enjoyable and fulfilling – if something has happened which makes learning a stressful event that adds to an already stressful life, it is not worth putting yourself through that.

Think about learning as something that can happen at any time in your life. If the time is not right at the moment, it will be right later. Postpone your course until your life situation becomes more favourable. Or stop your course and return to another later when you have more time available. Again, this is nothing to do with personal failure, but a good way to cope with an unexpected life event, as Malcolm found in the following example.

Malcolm (33)

I went on a course in the local centre. An A Level course it was. I always wanted to get a qualification and I finally thought I'd do it, you know? So I went one evening a week and it was great. I got on really well with the tutor and the other people and I was getting on well with my work, you know, handing all my essays in on time. Then my wife left me, just out of the blue she left me. Ran off with some bloke she'd met at work. I had no idea. We've got two kids and she left them as well. So I had the kids and they have to be picked up from school and they have to be fed and everything. I changed my hours at work and could get them from school but I couldn't go out in the evenings and 'cos I'd changed my hours at work money was tight, so I couldn't afford babysitters. So I had to pack my course in.

I was knarked because I thought people would be saying, oh, I told you so, you can never get an A Level. But my tutor said it were a real shame 'cos I'd been doing so well. He talked it through with me and asked if there was anything else I could do 'cos he didn't want me to finish. I couldn't do anything so he said he would get in touch with me next year and see if I wanted to enrol again. It made me feel better 'cos he gave me hope. He showed me I could go back to it when things were sorted and he made me feel good that I could get the qualification.

By the next year I'd met someone else and she has the kids one day a week. She's got A Levels and she really wants me to do it as well. I'm on the same course and doing well again, so fingers crossed I'll do it.

Life changes can come in many forms. Some are expected, some unexpected. As in the above example, it tends to be those which are unexpected that create the most havoc where our learning is concerned. However, you need to remember that just as the initial change has been un-expected, so can a change in the future which makes everything alright and possibly better than it has been. Malcolm's wife had been opposed to him returning to learning and had made it difficult. Although she had left him unexpectedly, he then met another woman who was very keen on encouraging him to return to learning. These changes had all been un-expected but had worked out well for Malcolm in the long run.

TAKING ACTION

If you encounter any of the problems mentioned above, there are several courses of action you can take to try to rectify the problem before you decide to leave:

◆ Prevention is better than cure! Before you enrol on a course, have a discussion with a trained advice and guidance worker who will be able to discuss your needs and steer you in the appropriate direction (see Chapter 4).

◆ Try to enrol on a taster course so that you can get a feel for the subject and the teaching methods before you commit yourself financially (see Chapter 2).

◆ Try to speak to your tutor before you enrol. Find out about other people in the class; ask about teaching methods and the required work commitment.

◆ Think about how you prefer to learn. Maybe you would like to try filling in a 'learning style survey', although you should remember that these forms are only as good as the person who has designed them!

◆ Discuss problems with your tutor – they may be able to

sort them out or offer suggestions about how they can be overcome.

◆ Discuss problems with other students. Often it is useful and reassuring to find out that you are not alone, that other people are experiencing similar problems. You might find it easier to approach a tutor with your grievances if you have the support of others.

◆ If you wish to continue with the course but can't due to some outside influence, find out whether it is possible to postpone the course and continue the following year when your circumstances may be more favourable.

◆ Find out whether you have already earned some credits that can be transferred to another course should you require it in the future.

◆ If you feel that you do not want to continue with the course, find out whether you will be able to get your fees back or transfer to another course without any financial penalty.

◆ If you have a real grievance, that is you think you've been treated badly or unfairly, find out whether the learning provider has a student's union. Discuss your problems with the education officer or welfare officer who will be able to advise you on an appropriate course of action. Or you could contact the Mature Student's Union or the National Union of Students for advice (addresses below).

◆ Do not think that you have failed if you have to leave a course. Treat it all as part of the learning process – you have learnt a lot about yourself, your learning style, what teaching methods you prefer. Armed with this information you can go on to choose something which you will enjoy and find extremely fulfilling.

SUMMARY

As an adult you should not feel obliged to stay with a course that is unsuitable for your needs. It may be unsuitable for a variety of reasons including:

- ◆ inappropriate teaching methods

- ◆ unsuitable subject area

- ◆ unsuitable classmates

- ◆ unsuitable work-load.

You may also find it difficult to continue with a course if you experience unexpected life changes.

If you have to leave a course you should not consider it to be a failure, but instead see it as part of the learning process and another step towards reaching your goals.

USEFUL ADDRESSES

The Mature Students' Union is an 'apolitical, self-funding campaign and support organisation dedicated to the equal inclusion of all students classified as mature'. It aims to promote the interests of mature students and act on their behalf.

Mature Students' Union, 6 Salisbury Road, Harrow, Middlesex HA1 1NY. www.msu.org.uk

The National Union of Students represents the interests of all students in the UK. Within the organisation is the Mature Students National Committee which works closely with the Mature Students' Union.

The National Union of Students (NUS), 461 Holloway Road, London N7 6LJ. www.nusonline.co.uk

10

The Benefits of Returning to Education

It would be wrong of me to say that *all* adults benefit in some way by returning to learning. However, I can say that in 15 years of working with adult learners, *most* adults I have encountered are able to list the benefits they have gained. For some adults the benefits may be small although still important, whereas for others returning to education has been a life changing event with numerous personal, vocational and/or community benefits. In this chapter each of these benefits will be discussed and quotations provided from adults who have experienced these benefits.

Although many adults cite the prime reason for returning to education as increasing their employment prospects and earning potential, once they have completed the course the personal benefits often outweigh the vocational benefits. This is why I have structured this chapter with career and earning-related benefits at the end.

INCREASE IN SELF-CONFIDENCE
For many adults the most important benefit they have gained as a result of returning to education is an increased

self-confidence. At first, returning to education may be a daunting experience – the system is unfamiliar and some adults have bad memories of education in school. As older people they feel that their brains may not be so active, that they may not be clever enough and may fail the course. However, they soon find that this is not the case – indeed many adults surprise themselves with how well they do on the course.

Increased self-confidence, therefore, may be due to un-expected achievements and success, but may also be to do with the fact that adults feel more comfortable about entering unfamiliar environments. On courses people get to mix with other adults – this develops their confidence in meeting and talking with other people. They get the oppor-tunity to think about and put forward their point of view which further develops their personal confidence.

Although increased self-confidence is one of the most popular benefits to be mentioned by adults, it is often some-thing that has not been thought about prior to enrolling on a course, as Margaret illustrates.

Margaret (57)
The most important thing that happened to me was confidence, it built my confidence. But I'd never have thought it, you know, it was just a small course for three days. I thought I might learn something new, but that was about it. I turned up at this college and I was suddenly scared stiff. I hadn't been in a classroom for

about 45 years. I just wanted to turn and run. But when I went to reception the woman was so nice and reassuring. She got someone to show me where I was going and to explain where everything was. Then I went to the class and met loads of other people. The tutor started by asking what we wanted to get out of the course and we all said to learn more. Then at the end she asked what we'd most got out of it and everyone said confidence. And it was true. You're put in this room with loads of people and you have to talk. In class we weren't taught like you are in school, it was all discussion, so you had to try and put your point across. I feel like I can do that much better now. I've enrolled on another course because I feel so much more confident now.

INCREASE IN SELF-ESTEEM

Closely connected to an increase in confidence is an increase in self-esteem. Once adults find that they are able to enrol on a course, enter an unfamiliar environment, chat with strangers, put their views across and succeed on a course, they feel so much better about themselves and their personal abilities.

Again, however, an increase in self-esteem is an important benefit that most adults report, but it is not something that had been expected or predicted prior to the start of the course. Indeed, some adults find that they are personally unaware of this benefit until it is pointed out to them, as Angela illustrates.

Angela (49)

About four weeks after my course had finished I was having a chat with my friends in the pub. Suddenly one of them says, blimey, listen to you. And I says, what? And she says you never would have said that before, you would have done yourself down and gone all meek and quiet. Now you seem like you're really happy with yourself and you're not bothered what other people think. Well I thought about what she'd said I knew it was true. Suddenly I was feeling better about myself, I could talk to them without feeling embarrassed or like I should just shut up. I'd been changing for quite a while and I hadn't noticed until she said. But looking back other people had noticed, like my boss had been praising me for my work – he'd never done that before. And my husband invited his work people around and he's never done that before.

INTELLECTUAL DEVELOPMENT

Most people enrol on a course because they expect to develop their intellect in some way. For adults this is of particular importance. Many worry that their 'brain cells are wasting away' or that they will not be able to 'keep up with the children'. Enrolling on a course is seen as a way to increase knowledge capacity and keep the brain active.

Intellectual development is an expected benefit and adults tend not to be disappointed. And since adults enrol on courses in which they are interested, they find it easier to retain knowledge and develop their intellect. Also, many courses, especially those aimed specifically at adults, are designed to draw out what adults already know. As an adult learner you have a great deal of knowledge and experience – courses help you to develop this and build upon it, as David found.

David (32)

I felt like I was stupid at work. I was mixing with all these people who'd got degrees and things and I felt I was the only thick one there. So I thought I would go on a course to learn as much as they knew, get the qualification and then knock them dead with what I knew. Most of the course was seminars and discussions – we would talk about our lives and what we'd done and achieved. We'd talk about our communities and what went on, then we'd look at government policy and how that was influenced by how people thought we should live our lives. When you started to talk about it with other people who were from similar backgrounds you began to realise how much you already knew. What they knew at work was different – it was just regurgitating stuff. They'd never been there, they didn't really know. So I was amazed at how much I knew; they just helped me to put it into words and arguments. What I learnt was that I wasn't as thick as I thought and that I can read *The Guardian* if I want to!

DISPELLING MISCONCEPTIONS AND NEGATIVE PERCEPTIONS

In the above example David shows how he was able to dispel the negative perceptions he had about himself as a result of returning to education. This is another important benefit which may not be considered or expected prior to enrolling on a course. It is also evident in the quotations from Angela and Margaret above – both had perceptions about themselves and their abilities that were negative – studying on a course had enabled them to challenge these perceptions and increase their confidence and self-esteem.

As we have seen in Chapter 7, adults have many negative perceptions or misconceptions about the education system as a whole. This is understandable when people have had bad experiences of education in the past. But the education system is changing and most adult education is different to the school experience. When adults enrol on a course they are able to challenge their misconceptions and find out more about adult education.

An important personal benefit to be gained in overcoming misconceptions is that adults are able to understand that other people with qualifications are not all-knowing, all-powerful beings, but just normal people like themselves. This, in turn, helps to increase an adult's belief in themselves and their own abilities, as Colin illustrates.

Colin (33)

I actually used to be scared of people with degrees, can you believe it? I used to think they must be so intelligent and so clever. I used to avoid getting into a discussion with them because I would think I would show myself up. Then I went away to university and did a degree myself. In fact I was surprised at how some students seem to have no common sense at all. They might be able to do the assignments, but when it comes to writing a letter, they just can't do it. So it really opened up my eyes. It showed me I was just the same as them, well, if not better really because at least I can write letters and I've got experience of the outside world. Some of the people I met just hadn't got a clue what it was like to go out and earn money. When I was their age I'd been working for five years.

PERSONAL GROWTH AND DEVELOPMENT

Linked to all the above categories is the issue of personal growth and development. Most adults feel that they have grown and developed personally as a result of returning to education. This might be intellectual development, as described above, or it might be a growth in self-confidence or self-esteem, also described above. Some adults, however, know that they have grown and developed, although they are unable to describe exactly how. Instead, they are able to see that they handle situations differently, or communicate with others in a different way, all of which is put down to personal growth. Others feel that they have been able to 'find themselves', and, for the first time in their lives, feel comfortable with who they are, as Liz illustrates.

Liz (34)

I think the thing I found most was that I grew as a person; do you know what I mean? I became more of me, if that makes any sense. I'm more like me now than I ever was. I know who I am now which I didn't before. I know this all sounds weird and it's hard to describe, although I know how I feel. I think I know my own mind now and what I want from life. Before I thought about others and what they wanted which made me unhappy. Now I can think for myself. OK it still involves others but we're all happier now because I'm happier.

DEVELOPMENT OF NEW INTERESTS

Many adults find that once they have completed a course they become more active and start to develop new interests which they had never previously thought important. For some adults this development of new interests is as a direct result of the course content – they are introduced to a new subject area which they find fascinating and want to follow up in more depth. Other adults develop new interests after having met and talked with fellow students – these may not necessarily be course-related, but might include widening social horizons. For others, it is as if a whole new level of life has opened up, with endless possibilities available for the taking.

Often adults are surprised at the depth and variety of their interest, and in the following example Roger describes himself as a 'sponge' that needs to soak up as much new information as possible.

Roger (55)
I couldn't believe there was so much out there. I was like a sponge, just soaking up more and more information. In fact I'm still like that now. I did one course and then I wanted to do another and another. And it's not just courses; it's introduced me to other things as well. Like instead of just going to the pub or a restaurant now I might go to the theatre. I've even been to a ballet and an opera. I never would've done that before.

MAKING NEW FRIENDS AND ACQUAINTANCES

As we have seen in Chapter 1, adults decide to return to education for a wide variety of reasons. One of these is to make new friends. If you are new to an area one way to meet people is to enrol on a course. Many adults do this and are quick to make new friends. It tends to be a safe way to meet people and you can spend time getting to know them and finding out whether you are compatible.

Although making new friends may not be the prime reason for some adults enrolling on a course, they tend to find that this is an added bonus. If the course runs over a long period of time it is obvious that you will get to know other people on the course, and since you have enrolled on the same course you will have that interest in common. Many people who have studied for degrees or other long courses stay friends for all their lives. Others find that they did not expect to make friends because of their preconceptions, but are pleasantly surprised to find that this is not the case, as Bill illustrates.

Bill (42)

I didn't know what to expect, but I thought they would all be cleverer than me. I felt like a bit of a fraud, like I shouldn't have been there, but once I went and started to talk to people I found that I'd been completely wrong. I finished my course three years ago and I still keep in touch with three of the people. In fact I've just become a Godfather to one of their kids so that shows how well we get on. I think it's because you all have to go through the highs and the lows together. You offer each other support and you live in such close proximity that you have to get on. But you're all doing the same course so you've got the same interests and you end up talking all night about some of the things that have come up. I think meeting those people was one of the best things about the course.

IMPROVED FAMILY RELATIONSHIPS

Unhappiness or a sense of being unfulfilled in our working or social lives affects our relationships with others. However, when we are happy and feel fulfilled, our family relationships improve. Although adults may not think about this benefit prior to returning to education, many mention it as an important and often unexpected by-product of the returning process.

Some adults find that unhappiness or stress at work leads to arguments at home. Once education has been used as a means to escape this unhappy working environment, the arguments lessen or disappear completely. Adults find also that relationships with their children improve – they feel more of an affinity with their children, understanding the stresses and strains which are placed on them within the education system. Some, as the following example illustrates, are able to get closer to their children through shared interests and concerns, so much so that it also benefits the education of the children.

Patricia (37)

I went to an evening class to study book-keeping. Courtney was 8 at the time and just trying to come to terms with maths at school. I'd been unable to help her before – I used to argue that maths had changed so much since my day that I didn't know what it was all about, but really it was because I was too scared to help her in case I got it wrong or showed myself up. So when I went on this course we would sit down at the table and do our homework together – we got support from each other. She loved having her mum sit down and work with her and I loved doing it with her. It made the course feel more worthwhile somehow. Then my husband would come home and sit and do his papers with us! It was great. And the novelty hasn't worn off yet.

INCREASED CAREER PROSPECTS

Many adults return to education in the hope that they can increase and enhance their career prospects, and many find that this is indeed the case. In particular, they find that opportunities have increased and that they have more choice available to them, as the following example illustrates.

Sean (29)

I was working in a factory and I thought I've just got to get out of here. I was working with people who I had nothing in common with. It was mindless work and mindless banter. It was so bad that I would go and have my dinner sitting in the car. So I thought I would go to college and get some more qualifications and get a better job. So that's what I did. I found it incredible how much more choice opened up for me. When I left school I went into the factory – there was no choice – that's what your dad did and his dad. All of a sudden I could look at other things, other jobs. It's like the city suddenly became a bigger place. All those jobs where you had to have a degree were open to me. I wouldn't even have looked in those papers before. Now I could look at stuff I thought I would never do. I got a job that was so much better in terms of what I did, where I work and who I worked with.

Some adults without paid employment decide to study for a degree in the hope of improving their chances of getting a job. This belief is backed up by national statistics. A survey conducted by the Institute of Employment Research at

Warwick University found that, in 1999, only 3% of people with higher education qualifications were unemployed compared to 6% of all those of working age. Although graduates do experience unemployment, the researchers found that this unemployment tends to be short-term. Also, the researchers found that employment levels are greatly enhanced by students on non-vocational courses enhancing their skills to increase their employability. Interestingly, it was discovered that employment levels of students from 'new' universities and 'old' universities are the same. This illustrates that those older universities which make it harder for adult entry are no better than newer, more flexible universities in terms of their graduate employability.

INCREASED EARNING POTENTIAL

The final benefit to be gained from returning to education is that adults increase their earning potential. Again, this personal experience is backed up by national statistics. In 2001, research conducted by the London School of Economics found that by gaining a degree a woman can earn up to 26% more than a woman who does not continue her education beyond A Levels. A man can earn about 23% more by completing a degree course.

A survey carried out for the Department of Further and Higher Education in Northern Ireland found that even one year's extra education can boost incomes. An extra year's education at any level can add 5% to male earnings and 12% to female earnings in Northern Ireland. In the rest of the UK, an extra year in education added 6% more for men and 10% more for women. Men were believed to earn an extra

33% a year if they had GCSEs than those with no qualifications and women could earn 28% more. And for many adults, this rise is so sudden that it is hard to believe, as the following example illustrates.

Adele (41)

I'd worked in schools cleaning mainly. When you do that you're always on the minimum wage possible, and you only do the job because you can't get anything else. Then I went and did a secretarial course and got a job with a local manufacturing company. All of a sudden I was earning three times as much for much easier work. I couldn't believe that change could be so dramatic and so sudden. I get on well with my boss and she told me she prefers older employees because they are more reliable and responsible. She's given me so much responsibility – I'd even say I run the company!

SUMMARY

There are numerous benefits to be gained by returning to education. The level and extent of these benefits depends on the individual, the course and the institution, and benefits will be gained and experienced in different ways. These include:

◆ increase in self-confidence

◆ increase in self-esteem

◆ intellectual development

- dispelling misconceptions and negative perceptions

- personal growth and development

- development of new interests

- making new friends and acquaintances

- improved family relationships

- increased career prospects

- increased earning potential.

Appendix 1
Applying for Government Higher Education Financial Support (England and Wales)

If you have received the offer of a place on a full-time, undergraduate course, you need to take the following steps to make sure that you receive the financial support to which you are entitled.

Step 1: Find out your Local Education Authority address and/or telephone number.
For the relevant telephone number consult your local telephone book. It will probably be listed under the main heading of your County Council, with a sub-heading Education – Student Awards and Grants. Many LEAs ask that you make your request in writing or specify a time at which you should ring.

Step 2: Ask for an application form (HE1)
This is a form that you have to fill in so that the LEA can find out whether you are eligible to receive financial support. The main criteria to be checked are:

- where you live

- whether you have been in higher education before

- your age

- whether your course is eligible

- whether your course is at an eligible university or college

- whether you are a dependent or independent student

- whether you are resident in the UK.

Step 3: Fill in and return form HE1 as soon as possible
To get support you must return your application form (HE1)
to your LEA within four months of the start of the academic
year.

Step 4: Receive notice of entitlement
Your LEA will notify you of your entitlement to receive
financial support and if you are eligible will send you a
financial assessment form (HE2).

Step 5: Fill in and return financial assessment form (HE2)
Some of the financial support you will receive depends upon
your income. If you do not want to declare your income, you
can apply for non-income assessed support and do not need
to fill in this form. If you want to apply for income-assessed
support, however, you will need to fill in this form. All the
information you supply is treated as confidential and not
passed on to third parties. This form must be returned no
later than nine months after the first day of the academic
year, but obviously the sooner you fill in the form the
quicker you will receive your money.

Step 6: Receive notice of how much financial support you will get

Once you have returned your forms, the LEA will write to you and let you know how much financial support you can expect and how much you and/or your family are expected to contribute. You will receive three copies of this notice – one for your own records, one to take to your chosen learning provider when registering and one which acts as your loan request form.

Step 7: Fill in and send off your loan request form

You must fill in your loan request form and send it to the Student Loans Company to let them know how much of your student loan you want to borrow. This form must be returned as soon as possible if you want to receive your loan at the start of term. However, you don't have to apply for the whole amount if you don't want to.

Step 8: Receive a payment schedule

The Student Loans Company will send you a payment schedule that tells you how much you will receive and when the instalments are due. The loan is paid in three instalments by cheque or directly into your bank or building society account.

Appendix 2

A Step-by-Step Guide to Applying for a Career Development Loan

A Career Development Loan (CDL) is a deferred repayment bank loan to help you pay for vocational learning or education (see Chapter 6). If you want to apply for a CDL you need to follow the procedure set out below. You need to be aware, also, that you are liable to repay your loan even if you do not complete the course through no fault of your own. This means that you should choose your course and learning provider very carefully. Appendix 3 will help you to do this.

Step 1: Apply early

It is important to apply early for your loan. The application procedure can take up to four weeks, and this may be even longer during the busy months of August, September and October. Also, it is possible that one bank may turn you down so you will need to repeat the application procedure with another bank. You can apply for a loan once your course has started, but you will not be eligible for a loan if there is not enough time to process the application before the course ends.

Step 2: Check your course

You need to make sure that the course is appropriate for your needs and that it will help you to achieve your aims. Appendix 3 gives advice on how to make the right choice.

Step 3: Make sure the learning provider is suitable

It is important to realise that neither the banks nor the DfES monitor or approve learning providers, even though the learning provider has to be registered with the DfES. You need to make sure that it is a suitable place for you to study because you will still have to repay the loan even if you do not complete the course. Appendix 3 offers advice on how to do this. If the learning provider is suitable but not registered with the DfES, staff can telephone (01928) 794307 for information on how to register, but they will need to do this quickly so as not to delay your application.

Step 4: Check that you meet the eligibility criteria

You cannot use a CDL for anything that is being funded by another source, such as a student loan or an NHS bursary. Also, you will not be eligible for a CDL if you have 'reasonable or adequate access to funds to pay for the course yourself'. To find out more about whether you are eligible for a loan, ring the Career Development Loan Information Line: (0800) 585 505.

Step 5: Check that your course meets the eligibility criteria

There are a variety of courses that are not eligible for a CDL. For example, you cannot receive a loan for a course that is specifically based on careers counselling or careers progression, such as CV writing, job-hunting and interview skills. Ring the Career Development Information Line (see above) for further information.

Step 6: Work out how much you need to borrow

When you apply for a loan most of the banks will ask you to calculate your monthly living expenses. They will also want to know for how long you require a loan. You need to take into account expenses such as books, travel, equipment and childcare. Chapter 5 covers these issues in more depth. You can borrow up to £8,000 or as little as £300, depending on your needs.

Step 7: Choose a bank

Interest rates, application procedures and the length of time it takes to process applications vary from bank to bank. The choice of bank is your decision. You can only apply to one bank at a time, but it is advisable to obtain details from all three banks so that you can compare the terms and conditions. You can walk into your local branch and pick up the relevant leaflets or contact the following:

The Co-operative Bank, Career Development Loans, The Co-operative Bank, PO Box 200, Delf House, Skemersdale, Lancashire WN8 6YQ.

Once you have been accepted on a course of your choice, you can find out how much your loan will cost you by ringing for a quotation from the Co-operative Bank on (08457) 212212. Written quotations are available upon request.

The Royal Bank of Scotland, Career Development Loans, The Royal Bank of Scotland plc, Drummond House, PO Box 1727, Edinburgh EH12 9JW.

You can obtain a quotation based on your personal requirements by calling the Royal Bank of Scotland on (0800) 121127 or by writing to the above address. They will need to know the amount you wish to borrow; the length of the course; the repayment period you would prefer.

Barclays Bank, Career Development Loans, Barclays, PO Box 228, Liverpool L69 7SR.

Existing Barclays Bank customers can apply for a loan over the telephone on (0845) 6090060. Other people will need to make a postal application. Further information is available on the above number for both customers and non-customers.

Clydesdale Bank. The Clydesdale Bank withdrew from the CDL programme on 15 October 2002. All existing CDL account holders are unaffected by the changes.

Step 8: Complete and return application forms to chosen bank

All application forms contain guidance notes. There are also telephone numbers for you to ring if you have any problems with the forms. Fill in the forms carefully making sure all information is included as this will help your application to run smoothly. Depending on the bank to which you have applied you may also have to fill in a DfES form and an additional bank form. The banks may need supporting documentation such as copies of bank statements or proof of your address.

Step 9: Complete and return the equal opportunities form to the DfES

The DfES is pursuing equal opportunities and requests that you help them monitor the success of their policy by returning their equal opportunities form. The information you supply is treated as confidential and not shared with the bank through which you have applied for your loan.

Step 10: Await a response

The bank will contact you as soon as your application has been processed. If you are successful you will be sent a credit agreement that you must sign and return. Your learning provider will be asked to inform the bank when you start your course – the money will not be released until the bank has received confirmation that you have started the course. If your application has been unsuccessful, you can try another bank.

Appendix 3
Points to Consider when Choosing a Course and Learning Provider

It is important to choose your course and learning provider carefully. That way, you will make sure that the course is suitable and that you will be comfortable learning in your chosen environment. For many adults who are unfamiliar with the post-compulsory education system, this is hard to do. However, if you bear in mind the following points, your choices should be made a little easier. It is important, in particular, to choose the right learning provider if you are taking out a Career Development Loan or having to pay expensive course fees. If you make the right choices from the start you will not lose out financially should the learning provider cease to trade or you find that the course is unsuitable in some way.

THE COURSE

◆ Does the subject area interest you? This is important to maintain motivation.

◆ What are the teaching methods used on the course? Will they suit your style of learning? Will they keep you engaged and interested?

◆ Have you met the tutor? Are they friendly and approachable?

◆ Who are your fellow students? Will you be able to mix with them, or will you have very little in common? Does this matter to you?

◆ How much work is expected of you, in particular, the amount of work you have to complete on your own? Is it possible, realistically, to complete the work, given other demands on your time?

◆ How long is the course? Can you commit enough time to complete a long course? Will anything happen in your life which might make it difficult to continue?

◆ How much time is required to attend classes, lectures, seminars and so on? Can you commit this time? Are there any extra demands on your time, such as field trips?

◆ How is the course structured? Are you required to attend regular hours? Will these stay the same or change over the duration of the course?

◆ What deadlines will you have to meet? Are they set by the tutor or by yourself?

◆ How is the course assessed? Will you have to take examinations and are you happy to do this?

◆ Is it possible to speak to any former students to find out what they think about the course?

◆ What are the retention rates and pass rates of your chosen course?

◆ What qualifications do you get at the end of the course? Are they awarded in-house or nationally recognised qualifications accredited by an awarding body such as City and Guilds (see Chapter 3)?

◆ What happens if you do not pass or complete a module?

THE LEARNING PROVIDER

◆ Is the learning provider registered with the DfES? If not, would staff be willing to register?

◆ Is the learning provider affiliated to any standards body (for example, the Institute of IT Trainers)?

◆ Are there any publicly available inspection reports which would be available for you to read?

◆ Do you know anyone else who has studied with this learning provider? If you do, what comments do they have? Did they find it a good course? Did they enjoy themselves? Did they encounter any problems?

◆ Have you heard anything about the reputation of the learning provider, either through friends and acquaintances or though the local media? If so, have the comments been positive or negative?

◆ Do you live close enough to the learning provider, or will travel costs place an additional financial burden on you? Could this create problems as your course progresses?

◆ What is the course fees refund policy?

It is useful to look upon paying for a course as paying for a product. We all know how to shop around for items we need and it should be the case with a course. We tend not to buy the first item we come across, unless we are fairly certain that it is exactly what we want. We also know how to look for bargains, whilst realising that sometimes we have to pay for quality. However, most of us know that it is not always the most expensive item that is the best. Shop around for your course; seek appropriate advice and guidance; enrol and enjoy yourself.

Appendix 4
Learning Tips for Adults

OVERCOMING MISCONCEPTIONS

Don't worry that everyone is cleverer than you – the chances are they won't be, but they will be worrying that everyone is cleverer than them!

Don't believe the phrase 'you can't teach old dogs new tricks' – it is nonsense. Research has shown that adults, whatever their age, are capable of learning great amounts of new information for all their lives.

Forget about 'not fitting in' – there are more mature students in the post-compulsory education system than 18-year olds.

DEALING WITH ANXIETY

Do not be anxious if you don't know something – no one will look down on you. Never be afraid to ask if you don't know. The chances are many other people in the class also don't know but have been too afraid to ask.

If examinations fill you with dread, choose a course that does not have exams. Many people have realised that written exams are not the best way of assessing a student's competence or knowledge and there are more and more courses available that use different forms of assessment.

Go on a course with a friend – it helps you to overcome your nervousness and offers help and support for your written work.

If you are very nervous or anxious about attending a course, find one that is aimed at adults like yourself. Have a look at the names of the course – often they will give you a clue, such as Computing for the Terrified.

VALUING YOUR EXPERIENCE AND KNOWLEDGE

Many younger students enjoy having mature students in their class as they can learn from their knowledge and experience.

Don't worry that younger students will do better than mature students – older people often obtain higher grades than their younger colleagues.

Don't be afraid of your own opinions – learn how to express them. Any good tutor will value your input, especially as others in the class can learn from your knowledge and experience.

MANAGING FINANCES

Do not buy every book on the reading list. You could buy some key texts if you wish, but your institutional library should have several copies of each recommended text. Remember that if a copy is not available, you can reserve a copy and it will be kept aside for you.

Rather than buy books new, check on college notice boards for books for sale. At the end of your course, advertise your books if you no longer require them.

When taking notes or printing draft copies of assignments, use both sides of the paper. It may sound obvious, but it's amazing how much money is wasted in this way.

Although college canteens may be cheaper than other food outlets, it is even cheaper to take sandwiches and a bottle of water!

READING AND WRITING

Don't read every book on the reading list unless you have the time and inclination to do so. Pick key texts and learn to skim-read the less important books.

If you are unsure of your writing ability find out about writing classes and seminars which may be run by your learning provider. You will learn some important tips and gain some invaluable help and advice from others who have experienced similar problems.

Some learning providers have study skills departments – if you have problems, join the department. They have been set up for people like you.

Ideas can be more important than grammar – get your ideas down on paper and if you struggle to express them correctly, ask for help from friends, family and your tutor. Many tutors with experience of working with adults will accept a draft copy of your work if you are worried about your writing style and grammar.

MAKING THE MOST OF YOUR TUTOR

On degree courses you will be assigned a personal tutor. This is someone who can help you with a wide range of problems and concerns. Meet your tutor as soon as possible; find out when they are available to help and do not be afraid to ask for help if it is needed.

Tutors can be very busy people and some may not have much time to spare. However, coffee breaks can be a useful time to talk – take the opportunity to get to know your tutor better.

Most tutors arrive early for a class. If you have something you really need to discuss, arrive early and you should have time for a chat.

Don't be afraid of your tutor or expect them to know every-thing. One of the most exciting things about teaching adults is that, as well as helping students to learn, tutors actually learn from their students.

Appendix 5
Useful Organisations

The Basic Skills Agency, 7th floor, Commonwealth House, 1–19 New Oxford Street, London WC1A 1NU. Tel: (020) 7405 4017. www.basic-skills.co.uk

The Basic Skills Agency is the national development agency for literacy, numeracy and related basic skills in England and Wales. The agency defines basic skills as 'the ability to read, write and speak English and use mathematics at a level necessary to function and progress at work and in society in general'. The activities undertaken by the Basic Skills Agency include:

◆ Developing family learning.

◆ Funding development locally.

◆ Awarding Quality Marks for basic skills to schools and colleges.

◆ Producing and publishing teaching and learning material.

◆ Exhibiting at conferences and exhibitions.

◆ Holding meetings, conferences and seminars.

- Producing a range of leaflets and posters.

- Commissioning research and surveys.

- Developing new approaches for ways of improving basic skills in schools, in the community and in the workplace.

The National Institute of Adult Continuing Education (NIACE), 21 De Montfort Street, Leicester LE1 7GE. Tel: (0116) 204 4200. www.niace.org.uk

The National Institute of Adult Continuing Education (NIACE) is the national membership organisation for adult learning in England and Wales. It is a registered charity and a company limited by guarantee. The main aim of the institute is to promote the study and general advancement of adult continuing education by:

- Improving the quality of opportunities available.

- Increasing the number of adults engaged in formal and informal learning.

- Widening access for those communities under-represented in current provision.

The work of NIACE includes:

- Advocacy and policy work with national, regional and local agencies.

- Provision of information and advice to organisations and individuals.

- Research and development.

◆ Organising conferences and seminars.

◆ Publishing journals, books and directories.

◆ Coordinating the national promotion of education and training for adults through the Adult Learners' Week.

The University for Industry, Ufi Ltd, Dearing House, 1 Young Street, Sheffield S1 4UP. Tel: (0114) 291 5000. www.ufi.com

The University for Industry is the government's flagship for lifelong learning and at the core of its work is learndirect (see Chapter 4). It is an independent body funded by the government. The aims of the Ufi are to:

◆ Drive up demand for learning.

◆ Engage new and excluded learners.

◆ Help businesses to become more competitive and effective.

◆ Help adults improve their employment prospects.

◆ Use ICT to make learning more accessible than ever before.

Glossary of Terms

Access course This is a course of study designed specifically for adults who are interested in returning to education. These courses tend to offer several different subjects within the course, so that adults can get a 'taste' for the different subject areas. The courses are designed for people who might want to go on to higher education. In some areas of the country universities have joined together with local providers of access courses to allocate a certain number of places on degree courses to students who have successfully completed the access course.

Access funds These are small funds of money available through institutions to help students who are experiencing financial problems. Applications for the funds are made through the institution.

Accreditation of Prior Experiential Learning (APEL) Adults enter college or university with a wide base of knowledge and experience. In some institutions this experience can be accredited, that is, credit points can be awarded to a student who is able to demonstrate what has been learnt from this experience. The credits can be used towards the final qualification. When you enrol on a course, ask whether your chosen learning provider accepts the accreditation of prior learning.

Bursaries This is an award of money to support study or

research. It may come from an educational trust or charity or from government funding.

Continual assessment On some courses, rather than have an examination at the end, the student's progress is continually assessed. This means that, at various stages throughout the course, the student has to complete an assessed piece of work. This might be a written assignment, a presentation or some other type of project.

Course A course is an ordered sequence of teaching or learning over a period of time. It is governed by regulations or requirements that may be imposed by an examining body or a learning provider. The length of a course may vary from a few hours to several years. Students may be required to attend a course at an institution or they can study on a course by distance learning, correspondence or various forms of flexible learning.

Credit accumulation and transfer Upon successful completion of modules (see below) students acquire credits. Many learning providers have entered into an agreement whereby students can build up these credits and transfer them between courses and institutions. When enough credits have been built up, the final qualification can be obtained.

Department for Education and Skills The new name for the government department that deals with all aspects of education and training.

Dissertation An extended project and report (usually around 10,000 words) that is carried out towards the end of a degree course. The student chooses a relevant subject, undertakes the research and analysis, completing the work by writing a report.

Distance Learning A course of study where a student does not attend classes at a particular institution, but instead interacts with a tutor via post, telephone, e-mail or fax. This type of course may also be known as a correspondence course.

Examination A formal test or assessment to test knowledge, understanding, skill and/or competence. Examinations may be written, oral, aural, practical tests or a combination of the above.

Further education Education provided for those over the compulsory school leaving age, below diploma and degree level. Further education colleges provide a wide range of courses – some are academic and some vocational. Further education courses can be studied full-time or part-time, during the day or in the evening. The further education sector, at present, comprises 456 institutions that range in size from a few hundred to thousands of students.

Graduate A student who has successfully completed a degree course.

Grant A sum of money offered to students in particular circumstances.

Higher education Broadly defined as any course of study leading to a qualification above level 3, that is GCE AS/A2 level and equivalents. Higher education study can be full-time or part-time and can lead to diplomas, first degrees, teaching qualifications and postgraduate degrees. Some higher education courses can lead to professional qualifications. Some further education colleges and adult residential colleges may offer the first year of a higher education course, although courses tend to be studied at universities or colleges of higher education.

Modularisation Many courses now run on a modular basis. This means that students study a number of modules that make up their course. Each module is assessed separately and credits can be built up towards the final qualification. Some students may study full-time, working on several modules, whereas others may study part-time, perhaps only studying one module at a time.

Postgraduate A person who is studying on a course at a level above degree, for instance on a Master's course.

Qualification A certified endorsement from a recognised awarding body that a level or quality of accomplishment has been reached by an individual. Most qualifications are awarded at the end of a period of study or upon satisfactory completion of a course. Some qualifications may require the completion of an examination, whereas others are awarded on completion of satisfactory pieces of work.

Semester Many learning providers, instead of having the traditional three terms, now operate on a semester system. Typically there are two semesters in the academic year.

Student loan A loan available for students to help with living costs. Interest on the loan is linked to inflation and students start repaying after leaving college or university.

Tuition fees In higher education tuition fees refer to the payment a student has to make towards the cost of the course. The rest of the cost is borne by the government. In 2002 the maximum amount payable was £1,100.

Universities In 1992 30 polytechnics in the UK achieved university status. Universities are independent, self-governing bodies that are able to establish their own selection criteria.

Useful Addresses

COURSES

Adult Residential Colleges Association (ARCA), PO Box 31, Washbrook, Ipswich, Suffolk IP8 3HP. Will supply a list of adult residential colleges offering short courses.

National Extension College, The Michael Young Centre, Purbeck Road, Cambridge CB2 2HN. Tel: (01223) 400350. On their website you can order a copy of their free *Guide to Courses* or browse an A-Z directory of courses.

National Open College Network (NOCN), University of Derby, Kedleston Road, Derby DE22 1GB.

Open University, Walton Hall, Milton Keynes MK7 6AA. Tel: (01908) 274066.

Universities and Colleges Admissions Service (UCAS), Rosehill, New Barn Lane, Cheltenham, Gloucestershire GL52 3LZ. Tel: (01242) 227788. www.ucas.com Applicant enquiries and application procedures.

Workers' Educational Associations (WEA), Temple House, 17 Victoria Park Square, London E2 9PB. Tel: (020) 8983 1515.

Workers' Educational Scottish Association, Riddle's Court, 322 Lawnmarket, Edinburgh EH1 2PG. Tel: (0131) 222345.

HELP AND GUIDANCE

Connect to Learning Network Centre, 3 Kingland Road, Poole BH15 1SH. Tel: (0800) 358 3888. www.dorset-careers.co.uk

Department for Education and Skills, Sanctuary Buildings, Great Smith Street, London SW1P 3BT. www.dfes.gov.uk

Guidance Council, 2 Crown Walk, Jewry Street, Winchester SO23 8BB. Tel: (01962) 878340. www.guidancecouncil.com. The national representative body for the guidance sector and, although not offering advice directly to the public, will provide names and addresses of guidance organisations in your area.

Learning and Skills Council, Cheylesmore House, Quinton Road, Coventry CV1 2WT. General enquiries helpline: (0870) 900 6800. www.lsc.gov.uk provides contact details for all local learning and skills councils.

Women Returners' Network, Chelmsford College, Moulsham Street, Chelmsford, Essex CM2 0JQ. Tel: (01245) 263796. www.women-retuners.co.uk provides information, advice and guidance to all women thinking about returning to education.

FINANCIAL SUPPORT

Adult Education Bursaries, c/o Ruskin College, Walton Street, Oxford OX1.

Barclays Bank, Career Development Loans, PO Box 228, Liverpool L69 7SR. Tel: (0845) 6090060.

Biotechnology and Biological Sciences Research Council (BBSRC), Polaris House, North Star Avenue, Swindon SN2 1UH. Tel: (01793) 413348. www.bbsrc.ac.uk

Co-operative Bank, Career Development Loans, The Co-operative Bank, PO Box 200, Delf House, Skemersdale, Lancashire WN8 6YQ. Tel: (08457) 212212.

Department of Health, PO Box 777, London SE1 6XH. Tel: (0845) 60 60 655. www.doh.gov.uk/hcsmain.htm

Department of Learning, Training and Employment, Student Support Branch, 4th floor, Adelaide House, 39–49 Adelaide Street, Belfast BT2 8FD. Tel: (028) 902 577 77. For enquiries concerning NHS financial support in Northern Ireland.

Economic and Social Research Council (ESRC), Polaris House, North Star Avenue, Swindon SN2 1UJ. Tel: (01793) 413043. www.esrc.ac.uk

Educational Grants Advisory Service (EGAS), 501–505 Kingsland Road, Dalston, London E8 4AU. Information line: (020) 7254 6251 (open Mondays, Wednesdays, Fridays 10am–12pm and 2pm–4pm).

Engineering and Physical Sciences Research Council (EPSRC), Polaris House, North Star Avenue, Swindon SN2 1ET. Tel: (01793) 444000. www.epsrc.ac.uk

Helena Kennedy Bursary Scheme, c/o National Extension College, The Michael Young Centre, Purbeck Road, Cambridge CB2 2HN. www.hkbs.org.uk

Medical Research Council (MRC), 20 Park Crescent, London W1N 4AL. Tel: (020) 7636 5422. www.mrc.ac.uk

Natural Environment Research Council (NERC), Postgraduate Support, Group Awards and Training, Polaris House, North Star Avenue, Swindon SN2 1EU. www.nerc.ac.uk

NHS Student Grants Unit, 22 Plymouth Road, Blackpool FY3 7JS. Tel: (01253) 655655. For enquiries concerning NHS financial support in England.

NHS Wales Students Awards Unit, 2nd Floor, Golate House, 101 St Mary's Street, Cardiff CF10 1DX. Tel: (02920) 261495. For enquiries concerning NHS financial support in Wales.

Particle Physics and Astronomy Research Council (PPARC), Polaris House, North Star Avenue, Swindon SN2 1SZ. Tel: (01793) 442118. www.pparc.ac.uk

Royal Bank of Scotland, Career Development Loans, The Royal Bank of Scotland plc, Drummond House, PO Box 1727, Edinburgh EH12 9JW. Tel: (0800) 121127.

Student Awards Agency for Scotland, 3 Redheughs Rigg, South Gyle, Edinburgh EH12 9YT. Tel: (0131) 476 8212. www.student-support-saas.gov.uk. For enquiries concerning NHS financial support in Scotland.

Student Loans Company Limited, 100 Bothwell Street, Glasgow G2 7JD. Tel: (0800) 405 010. www.slc.co.uk

ADULT RESIDENTIAL COLLEGES

Coleg Harlech, Harlech, Gwnedd LL46 2PU. Tel: (01766) 780363

Co-operative College, Stanford Hall, Loughborough, Leicestershire LE12 5QR. Tel: (01509) 852333

Fircroft College, 1018 Bristol Road, Selly Oak, Birmingham B29 6LH. Tel: (01214) 720116

Hillcroft College (for women), South Bank, Surbiton, Surrey KT6 6DF. Tel: (020) 8399 2688

Newbattle Abbey College, Dalkeith, Midlothian EH22 3LL. Tel: (0131) 6331921

Northern College, Wentworth Castle, Stainborough, Barnsley, South Yorkshire S75 3ET. Tel: (01226) 776000

Palter College, Pullens Lane, Oxford OX3 0DT. Tel: (01865) 740500

Ruskin College, Walton Street, Oxford OX1 2HE. Tel: (01865) 554 331

USEFUL ORGANISATIONS

Mature Students' Union, 6 Salisbury Road, Harrow, Middlesex HA1 1NY. www.msu.org.uk

Basic Skills Agency, 7th floor, Commonwealth House, 1–19 New Oxford Street, London WC1A 1NU. Tel: (020) 7405 4017. www.basic-skills.co.uk

National Institute of Adult Continuing Education (NIACE), 21 De Montfort Street, Leicester LE1 7GE. Tel: (0116) 204 4200. www.niace.org.uk

University for Industry, Ufi Ltd, Dearing House, 1 Young Street, Sheffield S1 4UP. Tel: (0114) 291 5000. www.ufi.com

Index